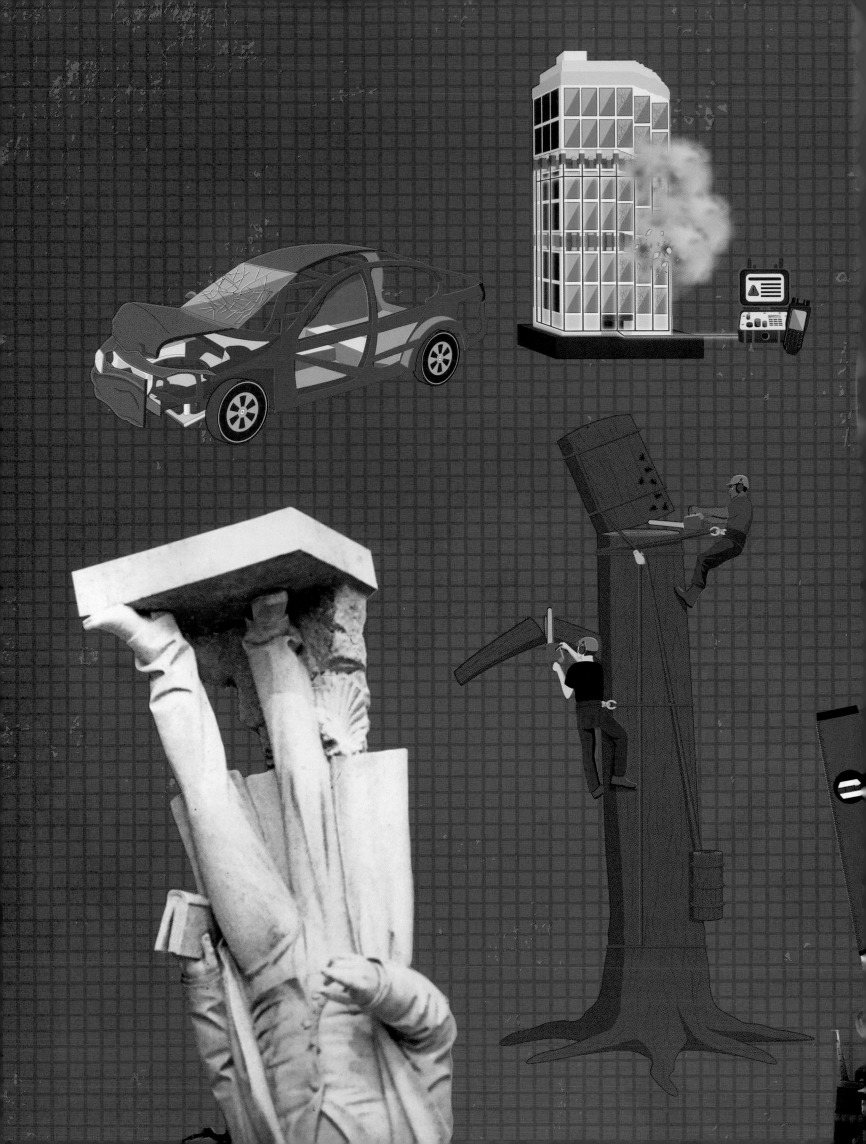

NATIONAL
GEOGRAPHIC
KIDS

BREAK
DOWN

Explosions, implosions, crashes, crunches, cracks, and more ... a **H⚙W THINGS WORK** look at **how things don't**

Mara Grunbaum

NATIONAL GEOGRAPHIC
WASHINGTON, D.C.

ARE YOU THE KID...

...WHO KNOCKS DOWN THE TOWER OF BLOCKS THE SECOND YOU FINISH BUILDING IT?

The sandcastle smasher? The first in line to bash the piñata? Don't get us wrong; knowing how stuff works is pretty cool. But what about when it *stops* working? How does it all come crashing down?

In this book, we're going to explore how things **blast apart, break down, wear away, smash, pop, topple, clog, and self-destruct.** We'll peer into the cracks of a smashed cell phone screen and stand on-site as demolition experts implode a colossal building, making it crumble directly into its own footprint. **You'll watch as mountainsides break apart** and investigate the most infamous engineering failures in history, from the sinking of the *Titanic* to

a tidal wave of sticky syrup that took out entire city blocks.

If you need a quick answer about how something falls apart, you'll find that on the "Just the Facts" pages. If you want to dive deeper, check out the "Tell Me More" section.

Along the way, you'll meet real-life scientists and inventors who analyze how things fail so they can learn how to make them better. They've helped make stronger buildings, safer cars, and products that protect against destruction and decay.

You'll also get a turn with "Try This!" challenges that help you understand the forces that break things down—and find ways to prevent them. You'll experiment, invent, create, and

explore. So strap on your hard hat, bust out your safety goggles, and watch for falling debris.

IN AN ACTIVE DEMOLITION ZONE LIKE THIS ONE, YOU HAVE TO BE PREPARED FOR ANYTHING.

WHAT'S INSIDE

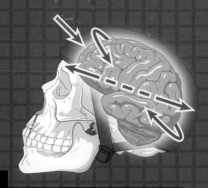

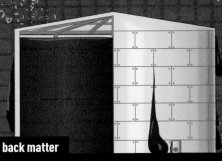

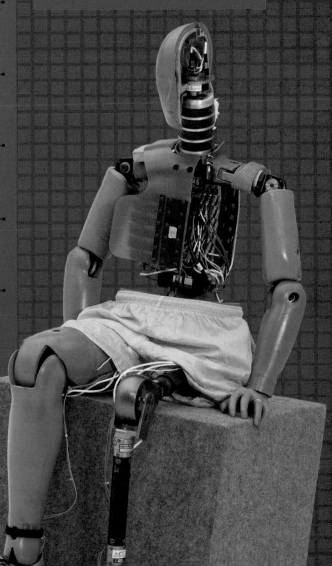

CHAPTER 1

ANOTHER ONE
BITES THE
DUST

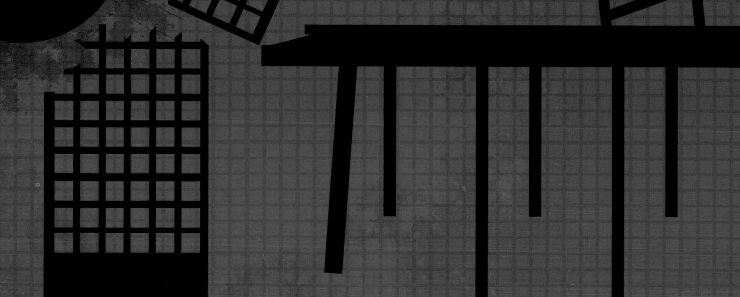

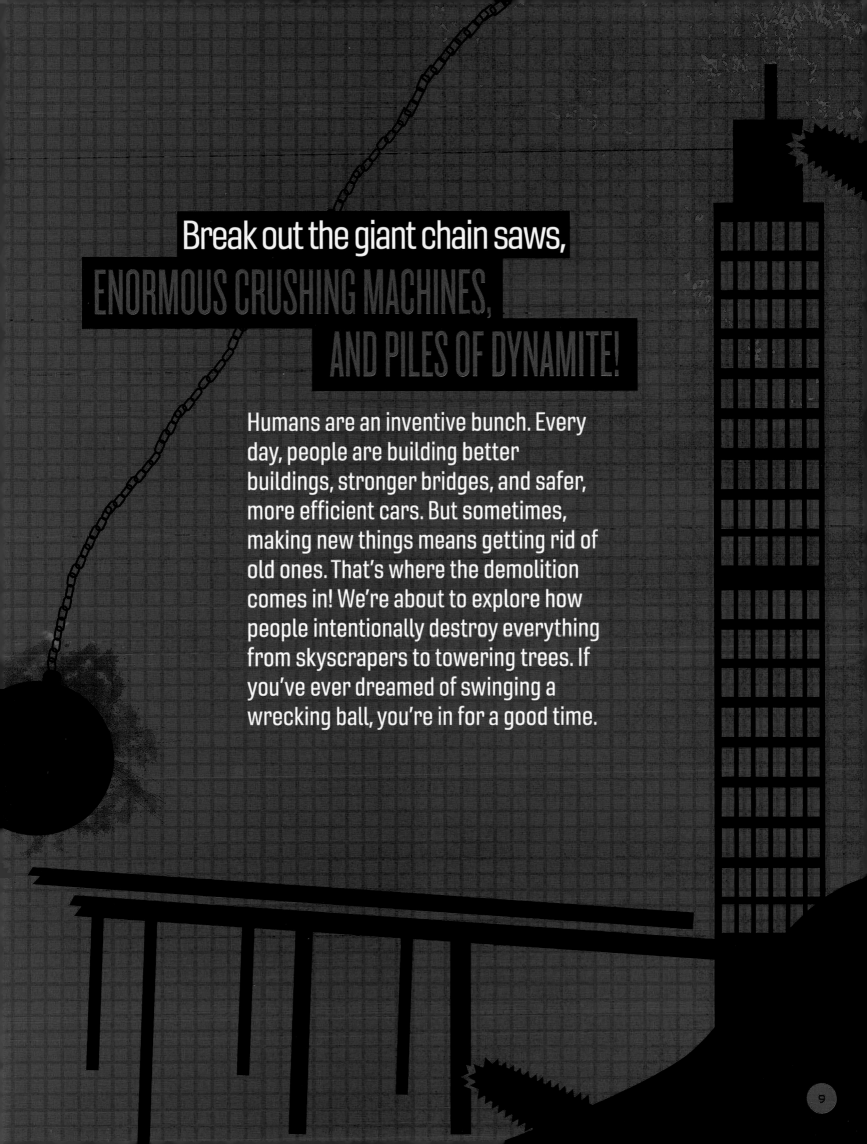

Break out the giant chain saws, ENORMOUS CRUSHING MACHINES, AND PILES OF DYNAMITE!

Humans are an inventive bunch. Every day, people are building better buildings, stronger bridges, and safer, more efficient cars. But sometimes, making new things means getting rid of old ones. That's where the demolition comes in! We're about to explore how people intentionally destroy everything from skyscrapers to towering trees. If you've ever dreamed of swinging a wrecking ball, you're in for a good time.

OUT WITH A BANG

How do engineers use EXPLOSIVES to collapse a colossal structure?

What's the best way to demolish an old building? Sure, you could use heavy machinery to slowly take it apart piece by piece. But where's the fun in that? We're taking a look at explosive demolition—in other words, blowing things up in a cloud of pulverized concrete. It may seem like chaos, but amazingly, engineers plan these events so a building collapses entirely into its own footprint. How do they do it? Let's find out: 3…2…1…BOOM!

Why do engineers implode a building ?

How do they control where it falls ?

How does it affect things nearby ?

Destruction on *purr*-pose is my middle name.

JUST THE FACTS

Controlled Chaos

Explosives like dynamite can turn a giant building into a pile of rubble in less than 30 seconds. But it takes months of careful planning to make sure that happens in a safe way. Engineers want a structure to implode—or collapse in on itself—not explode outward or topple sideways and damage buildings around it. This means trained professionals need explosives in the right places—and set off in the right order—to weaken a building's structure without spewing debris far and wide.

Blast Prep

To get a building ready for implosion, contractors clear out furniture and any dangerous materials. Then they break out the sledgehammers. They knock down inside walls that aren't helping to hold up the building. That leaves the concrete columns that support the structure. Workers drill holes in some columns and load them with explosives such as dynamite. When these explode, they blast cracks into the columns. Then gravity takes over, bringing a once towering structure crumbling straight to the ground. And if the job has been done right, it will all fall within the building's own footprint.

A building is demolished by implosion.

FUN FACT >>> One of the FIRST EXPLOSIVE DEMOLITIONS took place in 1773, when workers used GUNPOWDER to destroy an aging CATHEDRAL IN IRELAND.

BLOW IT UP

Carefully placing explosives within a building helps demolition engineers make sure the structure will fall in its own footprint.

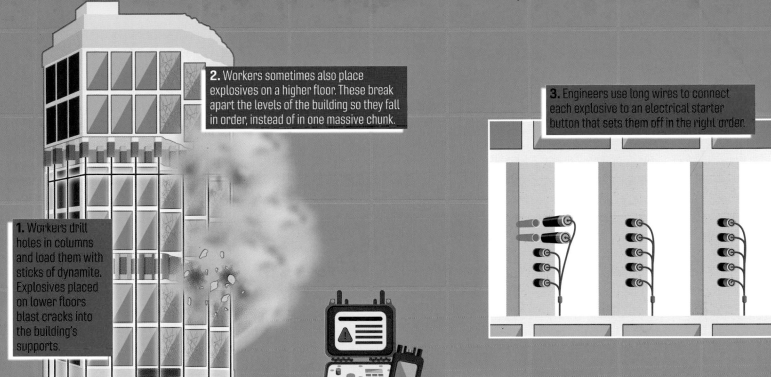

2. Workers sometimes also place explosives on a higher floor. These break apart the levels of the building so they fall in order, instead of in one massive chunk.

3. Engineers use long wires to connect each explosive to an electrical starter button that sets them off in the right order.

1. Workers drill holes in columns and load them with sticks of dynamite. Explosives placed on lower floors blast cracks into the building's supports.

Starter button

5. When the explosives detonate (or go off), columns collapse and stop holding up the floors above them. Gravity takes over, pulling the whole building straight down toward the ground.

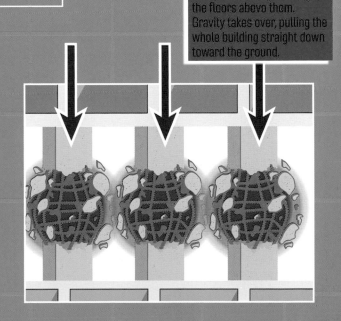

4. Workers wrap columns in chain-link fence material and sturdy fabric to keep debris from flying everywhere. Engineers also sometimes string sturdy cables between parts of the building to help pull things the right way as they fall.

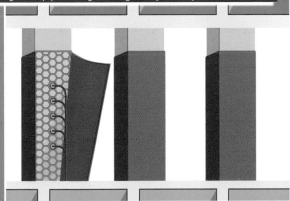

FUN FACT

>>> In 2019, a STATE LEGISLATOR in Massachusetts, U.S.A., raised MORE THAN $8,000 for her community by raffling off an opportunity to PUSH THE STARTER BUTTON.

TELL ME MORE

TIMING IT OUT

To plan an explosive demolition job, engineers first learn about the building. How tall is it? Are the support columns made of steel or concrete? Could other buildings around it be damaged in the blast? Based on what they find, the highly trained engineers decide where to place explosives. They also decide on what order to set them off so that the building falls exactly how they want it to. Spacing out the explosions just right also helps make shock waves less intense. These are the huge blasts of air that rush out of a building when all the air is suddenly squeezed out. An intense enough shock wave could injure people's ears and break the windows of buildings nearby.

FUN FACTS

>>> Fewer than **ONE PERCENT** of **DEMOLISHED BUILDINGS** are demolished by implosions.

>>> Director **TIM BURTON** filmed the **IMPLOSION** of the Landmark hotel and casino in Las Vegas to portray an **ALIEN INVASION** in the movie *Mars Attacks!*

>>> An **11-STORY BUILDING** can take more than **900 POUNDS** (410 kg) of **DYNAMITE** to demolish.

A powerful pile of dynamite sticks

TRY THIS!

Create your own mini shock wave using an empty cylinder-shaped salt container. Remove the metal spout from the container, then have an adult light a candle. Stand about two feet (0.6 m) away and hold the container with one hand so that the opening is aimed at the flame. Use your other hand to whack the back of the container. Did the candle go out? If not, move a little closer and try again. When you hit the container, you make all the air inside push out quickly through the small opening. This sends a shock wave with enough force to snuff out the candle.

WHAT A SHOCK

A building is about 85 percent air. As the air is pressed out in an explosion, it creates a shock wave that can damage things nearby.

1. Dynamite explodes by quickly changing from a solid into a hot, expanding burst of gas.

2. The large amount of gas slams into the surrounding air, setting off a high-pressure shock wave as air particles are pushed away.

3. The shock wave spreads outward from the site of the explosion faster than the speed of sound.

4. Windows too close to the blast site can be smashed in by the wave of air when it hits.

The windows of nearby buildings are at risk from the shock waves that radiate outward from an imploding building.

WHOA... SLOW DOWN. A CLOSER LOOK AT SHOCK WAVES.

Can moving air really break a window? Yep, and here's why: Even though you can't see it, air is made up of billions of tiny molecules. Each one takes up space. When something explodes, it creates a bubble of quickly expanding gas that pushes on all the air molecules around it. These molecules bump into the molecules next to them, which bump into the ones after that. This chain reaction continues, spreading the energy of the explosion out in waves. Think of it like dropping a shampoo bottle into a bathtub: The bigger the bottle, the more water molecules it pushes away—and the stronger the waves that radiate through the tub. Now scale that up to dropping in an elephant, and you have something closer to the power of the air pulsing out of an imploded building. Setting off a series of smaller explosions rather than one big one means less energy is blasted out all at once.

We've Got a Job to Do

DEMOLITION ENGINEER

Adrienne Loizeaux Grant was seven years old when she watched her father's engineering firm implode a 16-story high-rise in Boston, Massachusetts. The building was being demolished to make way for a big new skyscraper. About 600 explosives had been placed around the structure. "It was exciting to hear the sound of the explosive charges going off and see the building crumble to the ground in seconds," Grant recalls.

> ## " THE JOB IS NEVER BORING. "

Grant grew up watching explosive demolitions—and all the planning that goes into them. Her dad, Mark, runs Controlled Demolition Inc., one of the only companies in the world with the expertise to implode a towering skyscraper precisely into its own footprint. As a kid, Grant would hold her dad's measuring tape or hand him tools as he told her about how explosives worked. Once she was old enough and trained to handle explosives safely, she started helping set up demolition jobs.

Grant now works full-time for the family business. Its experts have been called to demolish office towers in Brazil; casinos in Las Vegas, Nevada, U.S.A.; and even power plant cooling towers in India. In 2000, Controlled Demolition used 4,700 pounds (2,131 kg) of explosives and almost 22 miles (35 km) of detonating wire to collapse a concrete sports stadium in Seattle, Washington, U.S.A. At 67 million cubic feet (1.9 million m³)—big enough to hold nearly 60,000 cheering baseball fans—it's still the largest structure by volume ever imploded.

Demolition work is extremely dangerous, so the company takes many safety precautions. Accidents on a demolition site can be a matter of life or death. In 1973, a piece of dynamite that hadn't ignited during the demolition exploded in a rubble pile Mark was working on. He was injured, and the blast seriously damaged his hearing, but luckily he survived.

To minimize danger, the engineers use only as many explosives as they need to weaken the building enough for gravity to cause it to collapse the rest of the way. In the end, natural forces do most of the work. But that doesn't mean it isn't fun to watch the destruction. "The job is never boring," Grant says.

Demolition of the Martin Tower in Pennsylvania, U.S.A.

Tools of the Trade

Demolition engineers choose their blasting equipment carefully. They want materials that pack enough punch to do the job—without making it too dangerous.

Dynamite

These blasting sticks are made of a material that can soak up a lot of a highly explosive liquid called nitroglycerine. When heated, the nitroglycerine molecules break apart and form a gas that explodes outward with enough energy to blow apart concrete.

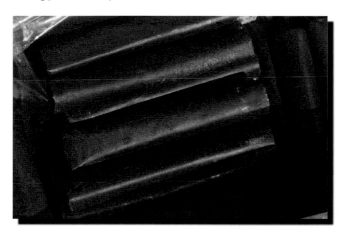

RDX

This white powder, also found in hand grenades, is one of the most powerful explosives available—it can pack twice the punch of dynamite. Engineers use it to blast apart solid steel beams.

Electrical starter

This battery-powered device sends an electrical pulse through the wires that connect to each explosive, causing a spark that sets off the blasts.

Delay devices

Engineers can add sections of slower-burning materials between the electrical starter and the explosives. This helps them control when each explosive detonates.

Demolition of the Tappan Zee Bridge in New York

WHEN **NITROGLYCERINE** EXPLODES INTO A GAS, IT QUICKLY **EXPANDS** TO TAKE UP **1,200 TIMES** THE SPACE IT DID IN A STICK OF DYNAMITE—BLASTING THROUGH **ANYTHING IN ITS PATH.**

CRUSHING IT

How are **JUNK CARS** stripped and smashed for recycling?

A car crusher has the coolest job at the junkyard. The big, burly machine quickly and reliably turns a pile of cars or trucks into a stack of flat pancakes. Why? When cars become old and not drivable, many of the valuable materials in them can be recycled. To be ready for recycling, they need to be totally smashed. So start your engines, because we're driving to the junkyard.

Why are junk cars crushed?

How does a car crusher work?

What happens to the crushed cars?

JUST THE FACTS

Space Saver

Why crush junky old cars? A car contains almost a ton of steel, which is too valuable to go to waste. But it's easier to transport car bodies to the recycling facility if they take up less space than they do on the road. A semi-trailer can carry three times as many crushed cars as whole ones. So after stripping off nonmetal parts and reusable items like hubcaps and steering wheels, junkyard workers send the metal bodies to be squished.

Pressing Issue

A car crusher squeezes the air out of a car body, crumpling it into a small cube or flat rectangle. First, workers use a fork-lift, claw, or magnetic arm to load cars into the crushing compartment. Then they turn on the machine, and a hydraulic (fluid-powered) system moves plates that press down on the cars with hundreds of tons of force. Some machines, called balers, also have side plates that press a flattened car into a cube. In about a minute, a crusher can flatten two stacked cars into metal pancakes.

WHAT TO SAVE

Cars don't usually go whole into the crusher. These parts are removed from the metal body before it meets its doom.

USEFUL STUFF: Any car parts in good condition—including the wheels, doors, or machinery such as the transmission—are taken out. Junkyards can resell these parts to garages or people fixing their own cars.

DANGEROUS STUFF: Hazardous chemicals, like gasoline and antifreeze, are drained from the car and disposed of safely. The battery, which contains highly destructive acid, is also removed.

NONMETAL STUFF: Worn-out rubber tires, fabric seats, and plastic parts like steering wheels are sometimes pried off to be recycled separately.

FUN FACT >>> In the U.S., MORE THAN 95 PERCENT of vehicles scrapped every year are RECYCLED, making them one of the most consistently recycled products IN THE COUNTRY.

CRUSHING MACHINE

Car crushers are designed to quickly and efficiently squish all the air out of a vehicle to prepare it for recycling.

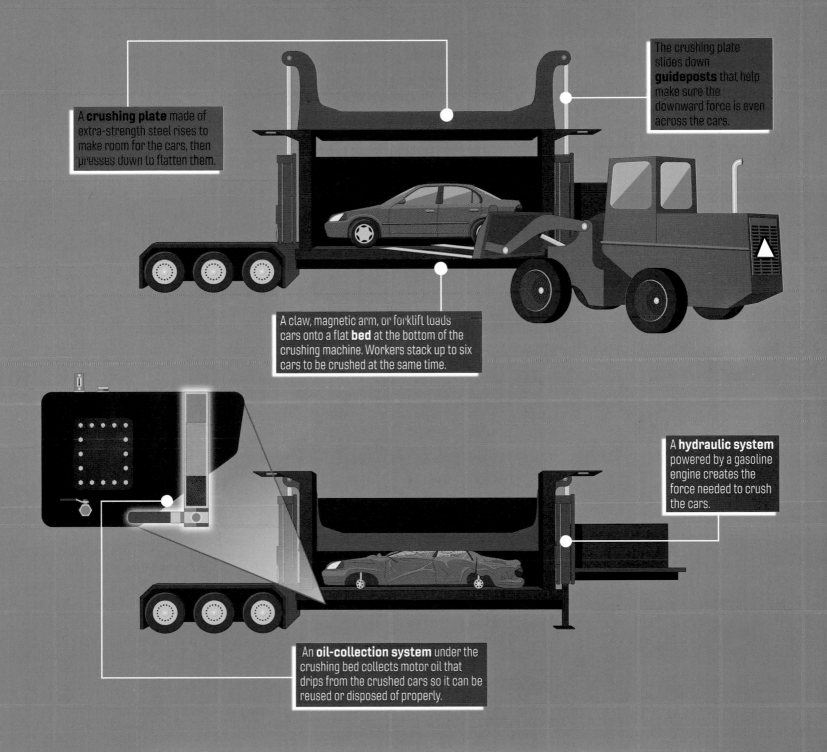

A **crushing plate** made of extra-strength steel rises to make room for the cars, then presses down to flatten them.

The crushing plate slides down **guideposts** that help make sure the downward force is even across the cars.

A claw, magnetic arm, or forklift loads cars onto a flat **bed** at the bottom of the crushing machine. Workers stack up to six cars to be crushed at the same time.

A **hydraulic system** powered by a gasoline engine creates the force needed to crush the cars.

An **oil-collection system** under the crushing bed collects motor oil that drips from the crushed cars so it can be reused or disposed of properly.

FUN FACT >>> Many modern CAR CRUSHERS are PORTABLE, so workers can DRIVE THEM to different parts of the JUNKYARD or to other sites.

TELL ME MORE

STRENGTH TEST

A crushing machine doesn't only have to hit a car with enough force to squish it. The crushing plate itself has to be made of a material stronger than the car it's trying to break down. Think about it: If you smashed a sponge with a brick, the sponge would crumple. But if you smashed the brick with the sponge, the sponge would lose again. The same thing goes for steel of different strengths, even if the difference isn't obvious from the outside. No matter how hard a car crusher pushes, it can't dent the toughest parts of a car body unless the metal it's made of is even tougher. So the crushing plate is made of steel mixed with other metals and heat-treated to make it ultra-strong. The result is harder than any metal in a car body. With this plate installed, a crushing machine can weigh more than 50,000 pounds (22,700 kg)!

FUN FACTS

>>> Car crushers are built **SO STRONG** that some of the first ones built in the **1970s** are still in operation!

>>> **A CRUSHED CAR** can take up as little as one-tenth the space it did when whole. Cars that are crushed into cubes come out about the size of a **MICROWAVE OVEN!**

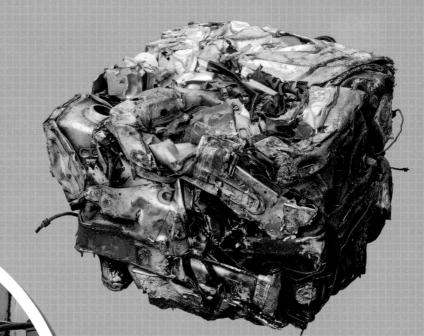

A freshly crushed car

>>> Unlike some metals, **STEEL** can be recycled **OVER AND OVER AGAIN** without losing its strength or quality.

>>> In the U.S. alone, an estimated **12 MILLION** or more cars are **CRUSHED AND RECYCLED** every year.

UNDER PRESSURE

The hydraulic system in a car crusher turns a small force into a destructive one.

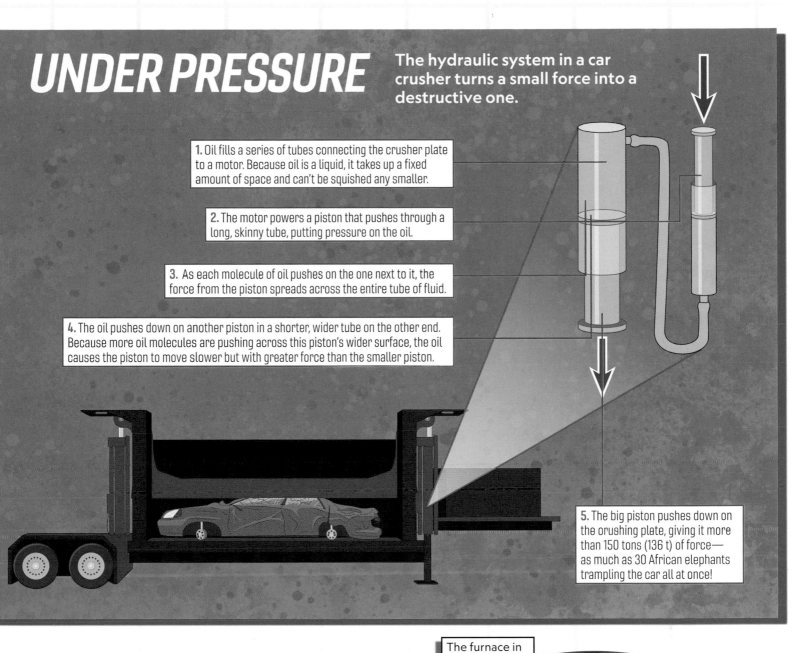

1. Oil fills a series of tubes connecting the crusher plate to a motor. Because oil is a liquid, it takes up a fixed amount of space and can't be squished any smaller.

2. The motor powers a piston that pushes through a long, skinny tube, putting pressure on the oil.

3. As each molecule of oil pushes on the one next to it, the force from the piston spreads across the entire tube of fluid.

4. The oil pushes down on another piston in a shorter, wider tube on the other end. Because more oil molecules are pushing across this piston's wider surface, the oil causes the piston to move slower but with greater force than the smaller piston.

5. The big piston pushes down on the crushing plate, giving it more than 150 tons (136 t) of force— as much as 30 African elephants trampling the car all at once!

PUTTING IT BACK TOGETHER

The furnace in an aluminum recycling plant

After they've been through the crusher, junk cars will never be the same. But they can turn into new cars—and that's often what happens to pancaked cars after they leave the junk lot. Crushed car bodies are sold to recycling processors. The pancakes are fed through a powerful shredder that cuts the metal into tiny bits. These bits are sifted and weighed to sort out different materials, like iron, steel, and aluminum. Then they're melted at high temperatures and re-formed into shiny new bars and sheets. Where does that metal end up? If it's not used in a building, odds are that it goes right back into another car or truck. Good as new!

TIMBER!

How do **WORKERS** safely take down a towering tree?

It starts with the whir of a chain saw. Then the thundering crack of wood splitting apart. Branches snap and leaves rustle as a massive tree trunk topples. *TIMBER!* Cutting down large trees is a dangerous job that's not to be taken lightly. But after centuries of death-defying work, the people who remove massive trees have learned how to use science and math to make it safer. Let's strap on our boots and find out how.

What makes a towering tree in danger of toppling?

What's the safest way to take it down?

What did loggers do before chain saws?

Time to Topple

Healthy trees stand tall and strong. But some trees that look strong on the outside are rotting and crumbling from within. Trees weakened by storms or disease could cause serious damage if they unexpectedly fell. Sometimes it's best to take a tree down before it falls on its own. Felling massive trees can be extremely dangerous, but trained workers called arborists have tricks to make it safer. They carefully manage the forces acting on a tree to control exactly how it crashes down. When there isn't space to safely topple the whole tree at once (like near buildings or power lines), the arborists take it down section by section instead.

FELLING A GIANT

Arborists carefully plan how to remove a tree based on its condition and how much space they can clear around it.

1. Arborists first inspect the tree for fungus and pests that can weaken the wood from the inside, making removal more treacherous.

2. One worker uses a harness, ropes, and shoe spikes to climb the trunk, cutting off branches with a chain saw on the way up.

3. Starting from the top, the arborist cuts the trunk in sections, since smaller chunks are easier to control.

4. Tree workers often use a system of ropes and pulleys to slowly lower the chunks to the ground.

5. The arborists continue working in sections until only a stump remains. This can be ground away with special machinery, treated with chemicals that dissolve it, or left to decay naturally.

TELL ME MORE

A falling hunk of tree trunk can be deadly, so arborists don't want to leave anything to chance when they're taking down an aging giant. Whether they fell the tree all at once or in sections, one big concern is controlling the direction the wood falls. They do this by using their chain saws to slice into the tree in a special pattern. They weaken the trunk on the side they want it to tip toward by making a notch cut. Then they make a much lighter cut, called a felling cut, on the other side. The tree will begin falling toward the side with the deeper notch cut. Once the top leans over far enough, gravity takes over. The force of the falling wood pulls the section above the cut away from the rest of the tree.

THE CLASSIC CUT

Arborists use specific cuts to control which way large trees fall.

1. The arborist makes the notch cut on the side where the tree should fall.

2. Then the arborist makes a straight "felling cut" opposite the notch cut.

3. If the trunk is leaning away from the notch cut, the arborist hammers wedges into the felling cut to push the tree in the right direction.

4. The intact wood between the two cuts acts like a hinge on a door, holding the two sections of trunk together as the top falls.

TRY THIS!

Can you control where a giant tree falls? After asking an adult for permission, peel a banana and hold it standing on one end—that's your tree. Now make your "cuts." Take a large bite out of one side (that's your notch cut) and a smaller bite out of the opposite side. Try not to bite all the way through! The banana left between the bites is your hinge. Does the banana fall in the direction of the larger bite?

IT'S KIND OF A FUNNY STORY ...

Arborists are usually called to take down trees or trim dangerous branches. But Shaun Sears and Tom Otto, two certified tree climbers in Seattle, Washington, found another way to use their skills beginning around 2009. Their tree-pruning business kept getting calls from worried pet owners whose cats had gotten stuck in trees. The two arborists—also cat lovers—decided to form a full-time feline rescue team. Now they use their rigging ropes to climb up trees and gently grab the stranded cats, then lower them safely. The arborists rescue hundreds of pets every year from trees as tall as 175 feet (53 m)!

SMASH IT UP

How does a WRECKING BALL smash a building apart?

There's something super satisfying about the high-powered smash of a wrecking ball. The operator pulls it back, swings it toward a structure, and then—wait for it—BAM! Bricks topple, metal bars bend, and another section of the building falls into a dusty heap of rubble. What's the science behind these orbs of destruction? Make sure you've got your hard hat on, because we're heading onto the scene.

Where does a wrecking ball get its power?

How do engineers move the heavy ball?

How does it break up a building?

JUST THE FACTS

Taking a Swing

The basic idea of a wrecking ball is pretty simple. A crane hoists a metal ball that weighs up to 12,000 pounds (5,440 kg)—as much as four cars rolled into one solid hunk. The crane operator lifts the ball and drops it on top of a building, or pulls it back and lets it swing into a side wall. Bricks and concrete are no match for the massive weight, and they break apart hit by powerful hit.

Simply Smashing

Demolition engineers started using wrecking balls widely in the 1930s. They remained the most popular way to take down buildings for nearly half a century. These days, the big swinging weights have mostly been replaced by backhoes and excavators—which can take a structure apart more precisely—or with the occasional implosion. But when it comes to satisfying smashes, the wrecking ball still can't be beat.

WRECKING BALL RELATIVES

Wrecking balls weren't exactly a new idea. As early as the ninth century B.C., ancient armies were designing ways to fling heavy things at the walls protecting their enemies.

BATTERING RAM: In this popular ancient weapon, a heavy log was hung from the roof of a portable shed. Soldiers used ropes to pull back the log, then released it to smash into an enemy's castle gate.

BALLISTA: The ancient Greeks and Romans used this slingshot-like weapon to hurl heavy stones at their targets. The biggest ballistae could throw 60-pound (30-kg) weights about 500 yards (460 m).

TREBUCHET: This early catapult had a long wooden arm that held a weight in a sling on one end. A group of people— or a box filled with heavy sand or rocks—pulled down on the other end to launch the weight into the air.

CANNON: By the 1300s, armies in Europe and eastern Asia were using gunpowder to launch hunks of metal rather than flinging them by hand. The blast from the explosive powder sent a cannonball hurtling out a long tube and toward its target.

READY FOR WRECKING

Wrecking balls weigh anywhere from 1,500 to 12,000 pounds (680 to 5,440 kg). Heavy-duty gears and cables help maneuver the hunk of metal on the end of a construction crane.

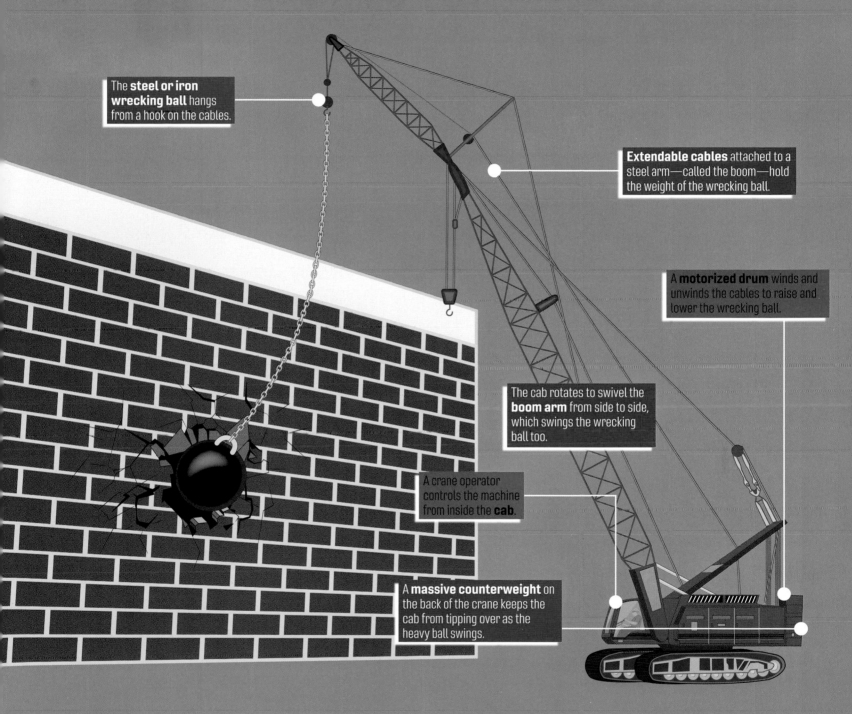

The **steel or iron wrecking ball** hangs from a hook on the cables.

Extendable cables attached to a steel arm—called the boom—hold the weight of the wrecking ball.

A **motorized drum** winds and unwinds the cables to raise and lower the wrecking ball.

The cab rotates to swivel the **boom arm** from side to side, which swings the wrecking ball too.

A crane operator controls the machine from inside the **cab**.

A **massive counterweight** on the back of the crane keeps the cab from tipping over as the heavy ball swings.

FUN FACT >>> A British company claims to have INVENTED THE WRECKING BALL in 1889 to smash apart an OLD SHIP. With only a STEAM ENGINE to help hoist the ball, the process took nearly TWO YEARS!

TELL ME MORE

MADE FOR DESTRUCTION

A wrecking ball works thanks to basic laws of physics. When the heavy ball swings on a cable, it's a pendulum—a weight that swings freely from a fixed point, like a person swinging on a swing set. As long as the length of the cable doesn't change, swinging the ball back makes it swoop upward. As the ball rises, it gains potential energy—in other words, the chance to release energy when gravity drags it back down. As gravity pulls the ball back down, the potential energy turns into kinetic energy, or energy of motion. The ball swoops forward as it falls. It has the most kinetic energy—and therefore moves the fastest—at the bottom of this arc. So that's the best spot for the ball to hit the building and use its energy to smash things apart.

>>> **WRECKING BALL** operators have to time their swings just right. If they **MISS THEIR TARGET** and the swinging ball doesn't stop moving, its weight could potentially **TIP** the **WHOLE CRANE** onto its side!

>>> In 1962, workers swung a **1,000-POUND** (455-kg) wrecking ball from a helicopter to **DEMOLISH A PIER** in New York City. They claimed it was safer because the chopper couldn't tip over like a crane.

>>> In 2007, a wrecking ball **THREE FEET** (0.9 m) wide broke off a crane in Pennsylvania. It rolled down a hill, **BOUNCED** off several vehicles, and injured three people before crash-landing in the **TRUNK OF A CAR.**

TRY THIS!

We can't tell you to test out a real wrecking ball at home—it would probably make your family mad. But you can still play with pendulums to learn more about how they work. In a clear area where you're not in danger of hitting or breaking anything, tie a metal washer to the end of a string. Next, make a big stack of coins and swing your wrecking ball gently at it. Did your stack topple? Play around to see if you can improve your destruction. What happens if your wrecking ball hits the stack at the end of its swing rather than in the middle? What if you make the string longer or shorter? What if you add more washers to the end of your string to increase the weight?

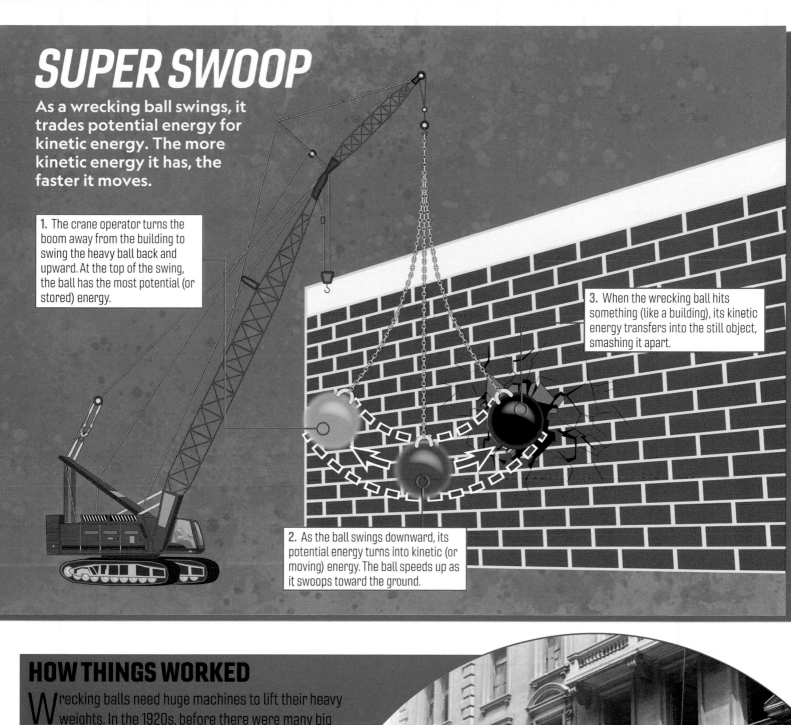

SUPER SWOOP

As a wrecking ball swings, it trades potential energy for kinetic energy. The more kinetic energy it has, the faster it moves.

1. The crane operator turns the boom away from the building to swing the heavy ball back and upward. At the top of the swing, the ball has the most potential (or stored) energy.

3. When the wrecking ball hits something (like a building), its kinetic energy transfers into the still object, smashing it apart.

2. As the ball swings downward, its potential energy turns into kinetic (or moving) energy. The ball speeds up as it swoops toward the ground.

HOW THINGS WORKED

Wrecking balls need huge machines to lift their heavy weights. In the 1920s, before there were many big machines around, workers called "barmen" did the dangerous work of tearing old buildings apart instead. Each used a wrecking bar—a five-foot (1.5-m) metal bar with a flattened hook on one end—and old-fashioned elbow grease to pry up floorboards and knock bricks apart. The work was hard and slow, and barmen weren't always paid well. When wrecking balls came around, they were a quicker and easier way to do the job. But there was a downside: With the slow, careful work of barmen, it was easier to save things that could be used or sold again. Wrecking balls make one big pile of rubble that's harder to sort through.

LESSON LEARNED!

DEMOLITION DISASTER
NOVEMBER 10, 2010

The Incident

It was a chilly fall morning in Springfield, Ohio, U.S.A. About two dozen people had gathered to watch engineers demolish an old smokestack at a power plant. Explosives had been loaded into the base of the 275-foot (84-m) chimney. Soon, a series of blasts would detach the tower from the plant, causing it to fall to the east into an area workers had cleared.

At least that was the plan. Unfortunately, it wasn't what happened. When the explosives went off, the smokestack started to teeter. Then it tipped and fell to the southeast—directly toward the power plant. Sparks flew as the falling chimney tore down high-voltage power lines. It crash-landed on a building and destroyed two generators as people scrambled to get out of the way. Luckily, no one was hurt in the accident. But thousands of people in the area lost power, and the plant's damage cost $19 million to repair.

What Went Wrong

After the botched demolition, the power company sued the contractors who had done the job. They said that the demolition engineers had made mistakes that caused the accident, like failing to cut the metal rebar that helped hold the smokestack together. Cutting it on the east side would have weakened the structure on that side, helping the chimney fall the right way. Instead, the power company claimed, the contractors used extra explosives on that side of the smokestack. But that only destabilized the tower, causing the base to collapse in on itself and allowing the rest of the chimney to fall in an uncontrolled way.

The contractors had a different argument. They said there was a crack on the south side of the chimney that the power company hadn't warned them about. This made the south side weaker and caused the stack to fall in that direction, the engineers claimed. The two groups eventually settled the lawsuit and kept the details confidential, so it's unclear who was most at fault—or whether both problems contributed to things going so spectacularly wrong.

THE BIG TAKEAWAY

NO MATTER WHO MESSED UP, THINGS CLEARLY DIDN'T GO ACCORDING TO PLAN THAT MORNING.

Even though there's no one clear culprit, there's an important lesson in this disastrous day. Demolition is more complicated than just knocking things over. To do it safely, everyone involved needs to plan and communicate extremely carefully. Many factors can affect how a structure falls, from its materials to its condition to the weather that day. People can't always predict everything, but the more information they have and the more thoroughly they think through the possibilities, the better prepared they are when physics does its thing.

DEMOLITION GONE

WRONG

THE SPRINGFIELD INCIDENT WASN'T THE ONLY TIME **A PLANNED DEMOLITION WENT POORLY.** HERE ARE A COUPLE OTHER UNIQUELY **UNSUCCESSFUL EVENTS.**

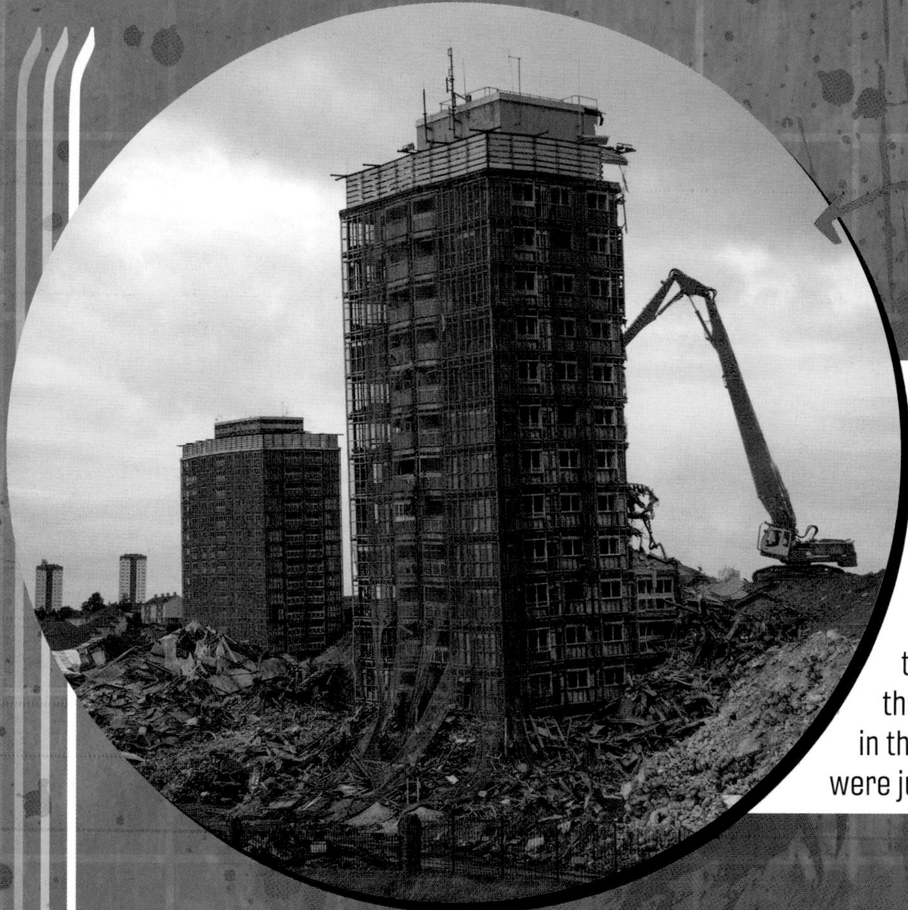

WHEN: 2015
PLACE: Glasgow, Scotland
INCIDENT: Housing towers

When it was time for Glasgow's Red Road tower blocks to come down, the demolition of the iconic housing buildings didn't go according to plan. Although four of the six buildings being demolished collapsed with no trouble, two remained partially standing. The contractor responsible for the demolition discovered that the steel columns used in the buildings were larger than what was noted in the city's records. It turned out the buildings were just too tough to bring down with explosives.

WHEN: 2017
PLACE: Pontiac, Michigan, U.S.A.
INCIDENT: Former sports stadium

Crowds gathered to watch a former sports stadium in Pontiac, Michigan, come down. But after the explosives went off ... nothing else happened. The blasts weren't strong enough to bring down the steel beams supporting the structure's weight.

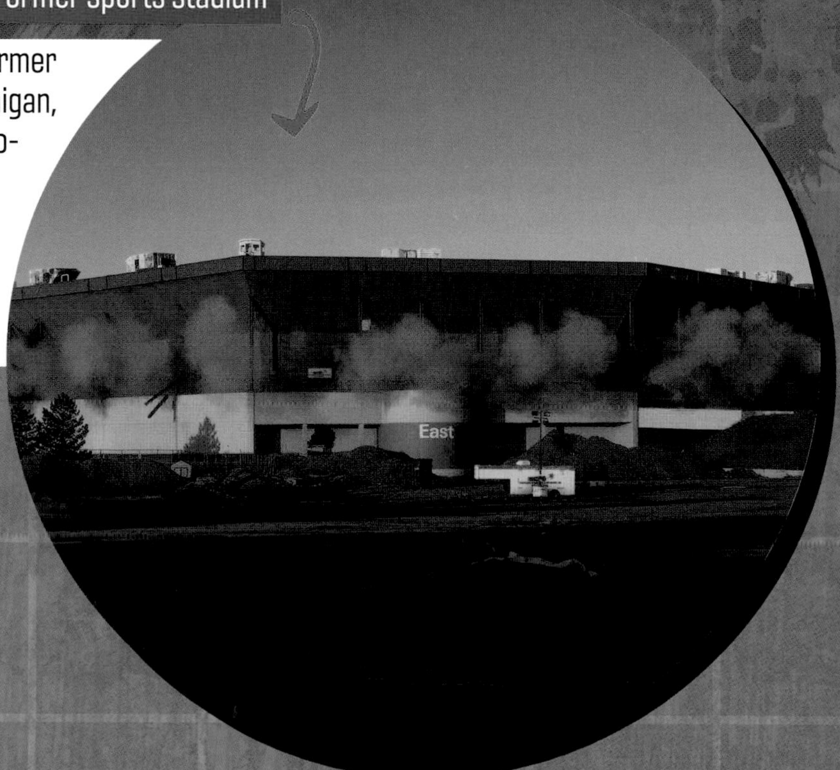

LOOK OUT BELOW

How do ENGINEERS take down a precarious bridge?

Bridges are awesome feats of engineering. Their builders balance powerful forces to hold up thousands of tons of concrete and steel. But just like anything else, bridges become old or damaged and need to be replaced. And this needs to be done before those carefully engineered parts give way and make the whole structure unsafe. How do you take down something that was such a huge undertaking to put up? Let's take a closer look.

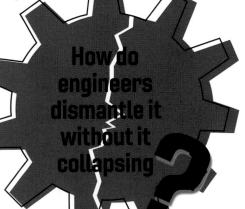

When does a bridge need to be demolished?

How is it different from destroying a building?

How do engineers dismantle it without it collapsing?

JUST THE FACTS

Breaking Bridges

Bridges are some of the most complicated—and dangerous—demolition jobs. Engineers usually want to take bridges down without dropping debris into the water or onto roadways below. This means that simply collapsing them isn't usually the best option. But gradually taking a bridge apart is also risky because of all the forces in the structure. One common type, the suspension bridge, has roadways hanging from tall towers on heavy, stretched cables. Disconnecting the wrong piece at the wrong time could make these cables fray and come apart like snapped rubber bands.

Tense Situation

In San Francisco, California, U.S.A., between 2002 and 2013, engineers replaced a two-mile (3-km) section of the Bay Bridge, which had opened in 1936. A piece of the bridge had collapsed in a 1989 earthquake. This piece was replaced, but the rest of the bridge wouldn't be safe if a bigger quake struck. To start the renovation, engineers built a new section of bridge alongside the old one. This allowed traffic to still pass through. But safely taking down the old bridge span would still be tricky. That's because some of the bridge's trusses, or steel frames, were under extreme tension, which is a pulling force. To keep the bridge from snapping apart, the engineers and crew worked slowly and carefully. It took four years to take the old span down.

WHEN A BRIDGE COMES DOWN

When taking a bridge apart, engineers have a lot to think about beyond the forces at play.

All that material needs to go somewhere. Four hundred fifty tons (410 t) of steel from the demolished Bay Bridge were donated to local artists to turn into sculptures.

The Bay Bridge demolition was delayed for six months while officials tried to convince hundreds of cormorants nesting there to move to spots they'd set up on the new bridge.

UNBUILDING A BRIDGE

Engineers removed the eastern span of the Bay Bridge in reverse order from how it was built.

1. Workers first broke up and hauled away the pavement from the upper deck of the bridge. This lightened the load that the remaining parts of the bridge had to hold up.

2. Engineers next dismantled a half-mile (0.8-km) section of the bridge called the cantilever. They cut the cantilever down the middle, then worked outward to take apart its steel beams piece by piece.

3. Crews then removed five 504-foot (154 m) trusses one at a time. Workers cut each truss on either end. They used pulleys to lower the five 2,500-ton (2,270-t) trusses onto barges, which carried them away to be dismantled.

4. Finally, workers used explosives to demolish the piers that had supported the bridge. They worked underwater at low tide to blast away the foundation sticking out of the mud beneath the bay.

TELL ME MORE

PUSH AND PULL

Designing a bridge is a stressful job—literally. The weight of a bridge deck, as well as the vehicles driving over it, put stress on the materials holding the bridge up. This stress comes in two main forms. The first is tension, a pulling or stretching force. The other is compression, a pushing or squashing force. Different parts of the bridge experience tension and compression, and the strengths of these forces change depending on how much weight the bridge is supporting. But the two have to be balanced for the bridge to stay up. That's why engineers have to take apart a bridge so carefully: If tension and compression suddenly become imbalanced, parts of the bridge could collapse or spring upward.

FUN FACTS

>>> Engineers removed more than **58,000 TONS** (52,600 t) of steel and 245,000 tons (222,300 t) of concrete from the old **BAY BRIDGE.** All together, that's almost as heavy as the entire **EMPIRE STATE BUILDING!**

>>> When New York City's **BROOKLYN BRIDGE** opened in 1883, many residents worried about its safety. The next spring, **CIRCUS OWNER P. T. BARNUM** led 21 elephants and 17 camels across the bridge to prove it could **HOLD THE WEIGHT.**

>>> There are lots of ways to recycle **DEMOLISHED BRIDGES.** Portions of the old **TAPPAN ZEE BRIDGE** in New York were dropped into the **OCEAN** for fish and corals to use as an **ARTIFICIAL REEF.**

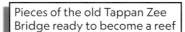

Pieces of the old Tappan Zee Bridge ready to become a reef

TRY THIS!

Stretched rubber bands are loaded with potential energy due to tension. You can tell how much potential energy is stored in a stretched rubber band by how far it flies when you release it. Find a safe, open place to launch your experiment. Using a few rubber bands of the same size, stretch and then shoot the rubber bands away from you. Try to keep your release at the same height and angle above the ground each time, but experiment with how much you stretch the band before launch. How does the length of the stretch relate to the distance a rubber band traveled?

BREAKING THE TENSION

To safely take down the Bay Bridge's cantilever section, engineers had to carefully manage tension to keep the steel beams from splaying apart.

1. The central piece of the cantilever section balanced on the archlike structures on either side of it. Its weight pulled down on the arches, creating tension on the steel beams holding them up.

2. To reduce the tension, engineers attached powerful mechanical jacks to horizontal beams on either side of the central piece. These pulled the beams toward the arches on either side, counteracting the tension that had been pulling the other way.

3. Once the jacks had controlled the tension forces, workers could cut through the central piece without the sides collapsing.

WHOA... SLOW DOWN. A CLOSER LOOK AT TENSION.

What is tension, the force that's so important when taking down a bridge span? Tension happens when something like a string, wire, or bridge cable is stretched tight by forces pulling on both ends. Imagine holding one end of a length of rope. As long as no one is holding the other end, there's no tension, and it's easy for you to move the rope around. But say a friend picks up the other end and pulls it tight, creating tension. Both of you can now feel the rope pulling against your hands, keeping you from moving farther apart. That's tension in action. In the case of bridges, this pulling force on the cables helps hold the heavy deck up. Why do engineers have to release tension from a bridge so carefully when they're dismantling it? Well, say your friend suddenly lets go of the rope that both of you were pulling on. The sudden release of tension might knock you over—and the harder you'd been pulling, the worse this effect would be.

TRY THIS!

DA VINCI BRIDGE

He painted the "Mona Lisa." He designed a flying machine hundreds of years before airplanes were invented. Was there anything Leonardo da Vinci couldn't do? This craft-stick bridge based on one of his sketches may look flimsy, but it's no toothpick. Leonardo understood that if you use natural forces as a tool, you don't necessarily need fancy fasteners and sticky adhesives. That's right, this bridge has no glue, no screws, no rubber bands ... nothing to hold it together except friction and tension.

WHAT YOU NEED

TIME: About 30 to 45 minutes

It can help to have an extra set of hands for this experiment—weaving the craft sticks in place can get a bit tricky.

1. 12 craft sticks (or more if you're feeling bold)

2. Pen

3. A flat, stable workspace

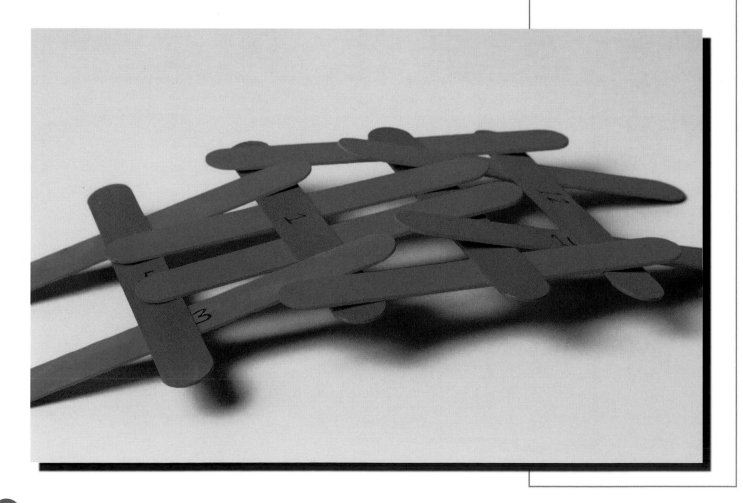

42

1. Use your pen to number your craft sticks (1–12, or however many you're using). Put stick 1 in the center of your workspace. Place sticks 2 and 3 perpendicular to stick 1 and overlapping it slightly. They should be spaced evenly apart from each other about a third from each end.

2. Now place stick 4 over sticks 2 and 3, about 1 inch (2.5 cm) from stick 1.

3. Using one hand to hold stick 4 in place, gently slide sticks 5 and 6 under stick 1 from the right so that they are next to each other, then have them overlap stick 4.

4. Keeping a steadying hand on stick 4, slide stick 7 underneath sticks 5 and 6. Now weave stick 8 under the top edge of stick 7, then over the tip of stick 1. Repeat with stick 9 on the bottom.

5. Your bridge should begin to rise into the air! Use one hand to press it flat to make it easier to add to your construction.

6. Place sticks 10 and 11 over stick 7. They should fall between sticks 8 and 9 on the outside and sticks 5 and 6 on the inside.

7. Now slide stick 12 over sticks 10 and 11 and under sticks 8 and 9.

8. You can continue building your bridge into a higher arch by weaving a new stick first vertically under the farthest sticks to the right, then adding two more horizontally under the newest vertical stick, then over the next vertical stick in line to the left.

9. Once it's as high as you want it to be, start piling on items to see how much weight it can support before buckling.

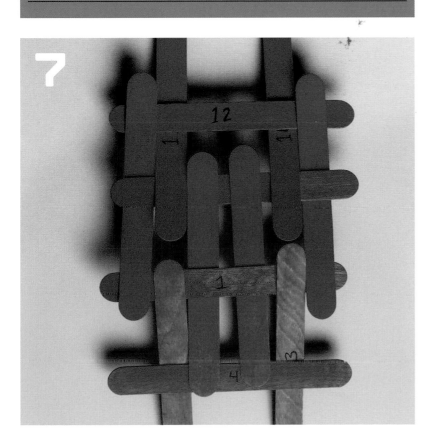

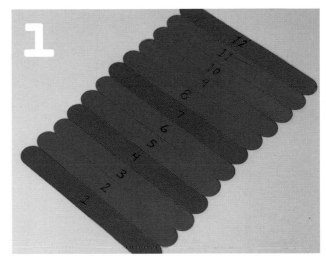

 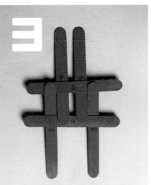

WHAT TO EXPECT

THE BRIDGE SHOULD SUPPORT QUITE A BIT OF WEIGHT. IN FACT, IT WILL LIKELY PRESS FLAT BEFORE IT BREAKS. BUT REMOVING JUST ONE STICK OR PUSHING THE BRIDGE FROM THE SIDE CAN DESTABILIZE THE WHOLE STRUCTURE, AND THE BRIDGE COMES CRASHING DOWN.

WHAT'S GOING ON?

BY WEAVING THE CRAFT STICKS UNDER AND OVER ONE ANOTHER, YOU CREATE FRICTION AND TENSION BETWEEN THE STICKS THAT PREVENT THEM FROM MOVING. WHEN YOU PLACE OBJECTS ON THE BRIDGE, THE DOWNWARD PRESSURE FROM THIS WEIGHT PRESSES EVEN MORE ON THE STICKS, WHICH FURTHER STRENGTHENS THE FRICTION AND TENSION. REMOVING A STICK, HOWEVER, RELEASES TENSION, AND ONCE A STICK STARTS TO SLIDE OUT OF PLACE IN ONE SPOT, THE FRICTION BETWEEN THE REST OF THE STICKS ISN'T STRONG ENOUGH TO BALANCE OUT THE FORCE OF GRAVITY PULLING DOWN ON THEM. CRASH!

CHAPTER 2

BUILT TO BREAK

The things we use should be built to last, right? BUT SOMETIMES FALLING APART ISN'T A FLAW—IT'S A FEATURE.

You heard that right: Scientists and engineers have found clever ways to harness the forces of chaos to help us. It's how fireworks entertain us, fuses keep our homes safe, and bike helmets protect us in a crash. Check out the technologies big and small that break and blow themselves up for our benefit. It'll be a blast!

CRASH COMPACTOR

How does a **CAR'S DESIGN** protect you in an accident?

An indestructible car sounds cool, right? And sure, that'd be great, if the car itself were the only thing you needed to worry about in a crash. But just as important as taking us where we need to go, a car needs to protect us in the unfortunate event of an accident. That's why cars are intentionally designed to take some damage instead of their drivers and passengers. But how does breaking make cars safer? Buckle up, and let's find out.

What are cars made of ?

What happens when they crash ?

How does their structure protect people ?

I'm nobody's dummy!

FO4305OZ02

JUST THE FACTS

Crumple Up

If a car's hood is bent out of shape after an accident, it may look like the car was poorly made. But in many cases, this smashed hood is a sign that the car was doing its job. In the early 1900s, as driving became more common, people thought car bodies should be as rigid as possible. These boxy designs might have survived accidents—but the people inside them often did not. In the 1950s, engineers realized that designing certain parts of cars to crush more easily would actually save passengers' lives. And so, the crumple zone was born.

Force Factor

Here's the basic idea: The faster a moving car stops—and the faster it was going before then—the more force is felt inside it. (Think about the difference you feel when a driver slams on the brakes versus gradually slowing down for a red light.) A car in an accident can go from cruising down the highway to being stopped almost instantaneously, and the energy from the stop has to go somewhere. It spreads through the car's frame, then into its passenger compartment, then into the passengers themselves, throwing them around inside the vehicle. Enter the crumple zone. By being designed to collapse under impact instead of staying rigid, a crumple zone absorbs much of the energy of a crash. By the time the effects of the impact reach the passengers, there's less energy to injure them.

BETTER BODIES

In 2009, engineers crash-tested a modern Chevrolet against one from the late 1950s. The results show just how much car safety standards have improved.

NEW CARS: When the two cars crashed, the hood of the modern car crumpled. But the driver's compartment kept its shape, meaning a real driver likely would have been OK.

OLD CARS: A driver in the old car wouldn't have been so lucky. Its bulky frame collapsed around the passenger area, squishing the crash-test dummy in its seat.

PROTECTION ZONES

Different parts of a car's body are designed to absorb energy from accidents. Here's how they work together to protect passengers in a crash.

Safety zone: A "safety cage" around a car's passenger compartment is made of strengthened steel. It can take a lot of force without changing shape, keeping the driver and passenger areas from being crushed.

Frontline defense: The hood and bumper make up parts of a car's front crumple zone. When something hits the front of the car, materials like aluminum and flexible steel bend to absorb the impact.

Rear guard: A second crumple zone in the back protects passengers if the car is rear-ended. The groceries in the trunk might be damaged—but better that than the people inside.

Side-crash safety: Extra-tough bars across the doors of some cars keep the doors from collapsing inward if something hits the side of the car.

FUN FACT

>>> The luxury car company MERCEDES-BENZ was the first to make cars with CRUMPLE ZONES in the 1950s.

Cars have come a long way since their dangerous early days. Modern models have dozens of features with one goal: to keep the force of a crash from hurting the people inside. In addition to crumple zones, many cars have a steering column that collapses to absorb energy if the driver slams into it. Airbags inflate in an instant to cushion the head and neck in a crash. Seat belts slow your body down when the force of a sudden stop throws it forward. And safety glass doesn't shatter into sharp pieces, reducing the risk of nasty cuts. Of course, drivers still need to do everything they can to avoid accidents. But the odds of surviving one are now far better than they were even 45 years ago.

FUN FACTS

>>> Connecticut was the first U.S. state to make **TRAFFIC LAWS.** In 1901, it set the speed limit within cities at **12 MILES AN HOUR** (19 km/h).

>>> **SAFETY GLASS** is also used in computer screens, oven doors, and eyeglasses—all places where **SHATTERING GLASS** could be particularly disastrous.

>>> A **CHEMICAL REACTION** inside an airbag fills it up with gas in less than **ONE-TWENTIETH** of a second after a crash.

>>> Carmakers in **SWEDEN** use **790-POUND** (360-kg) moose dummies to test how their cars hold up to hitting the **ANIMALS** in the road.

SPEED LIMIT 12

TRY THIS!

What household items make the best crumple zone for a toy car? Use a rubber band to attach different materials to a small wheeled toy. Try crumpled-up tinfoil, marshmallows, a cotton ball or clean tissues, and anything else you think might do the job—even a crumpled-up pair of clean socks! Now ask an adult to help you find a spot where you can push the car toward a wall without doing any damage. Which material works best to absorb force and stop the car smoothly (without it bouncing back from the wall or flipping over)?

SUPER SHIELDS

Sharp flying glass is the last thing you need in a car accident. That's why car windows are made of safety glass—toughened material designed to break without creating knifelike shards.

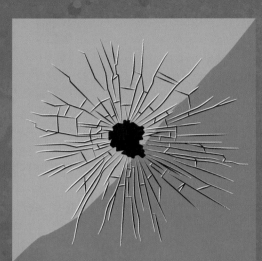

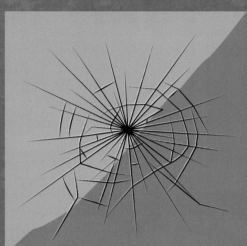

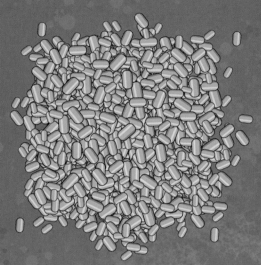

UNTREATED GLASS: Normal glass, like you see in jars and beverage bottles, breaks into jagged pieces. It's not used in cars because it can easily cut people when it breaks.

LAMINATED GLASS: A car's front windshield is made of two panes of glass sandwiched around a clear layer of sticky plastic. If the glass breaks, the sticky layer holds the pieces in place.

TEMPERED GLASS: The glass used for side and rear windows has been heated to about 1200 degrees Fahrenheit (650°C) and then cooled again. This process strengthens the glass and forces it to split into small, rounded pieces instead of shards if it breaks.

PUTTING IT BACK TOGETHER

Cars can look gnarly after an accident. But some of the damage is easier to fix than you might expect. The flexibility of the metal means handheld tools like suction cups can pull out minor dents in a car's body. Heavier machinery in an auto shop can sometimes pull and bend a misshapen frame back into its original shape. Windshields and side windows can be replaced. But depending on how serious the accident was, these repairs may or may not be worth it. If repairing the car would cost more than it's worth—or the reshaped frame wouldn't be safe in another crash—then the car is considered totaled and is destined for the junkyard.

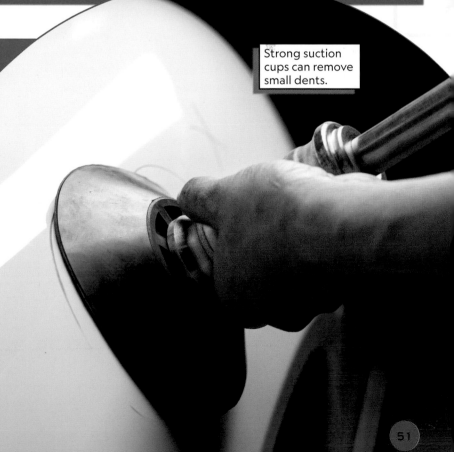

Strong suction cups can remove small dents.

We've Got a Job to Do

Most of us don't want to be anywhere near a car accident. But Becky Mueller makes them happen on purpose roughly twice a week. Mueller is an engineer at the Insurance Institute for Highway Safety (IIHS) in Ruckersville, Virginia, U.S.A. She designs crash tests that help the IIHS rate the safety of different vehicles.

> ## " WHO DOESN'T WANT TO GET PAID TO BREAK STUFF? "

Mueller was obsessed with cars as a kid. She also knew she wanted a job that helped people. In college, she studied engineering and biomechanics—the science of how the human body moves. Soon after, she landed her dream job as an engineer at the IIHS.

To plan a crash test, Mueller studies real-world car accidents. She asks questions like, What kinds of crashes are the most dangerous to people? Then she designs a test to simulate these conditions. For example, she might want a car to swipe another car along one side or to crash head-on into a wall.

The IIHS buys cars from the same dealers that regular people do. Technicians spend days preparing each one for its test. They install cameras and sensors and load in a crash-test dummy to stand in for a human driver or passenger. Then they attach the car to a pulley system in the floor of a giant warehouse.

The pulleys pull the car to speed it up, then release it to slam into a barrier. Mueller and her colleagues watch from a platform, safe from flying debris. The crash is over in 200 milliseconds—about as long as a single blink takes. But high-speed cameras film from every angle so engineers can watch it in slow motion afterward.

After the crash, technicians measure how much different parts of the car were damaged. Sensors in the dummy report the forces it experienced. This tells the engineers how likely someone is to get an injury. Carmakers can use this information to make their vehicles safer in a real crash, and customers use it when deciding which car to buy.

Mueller takes keeping people safe extremely seriously. But engineering crash tests is also a lot of fun. "Who doesn't want to get paid to break stuff?" Mueller explains. "Every single test is exciting for me."

TECHNICIANS SOMETIMES SMEAR A DUMMY'S FACE WITH **PAINT** BEFORE A **CRASH TEST.** THE PAINT **RUBS OFF** WHEN IT TOUCHES THE **CAR'S AIRBAG,** SHOWING ANALYSTS WHERE THE DUMMY'S HEAD HIT.

Thanks, Dummies!

Crash-test dummies are designed to survive hundreds of high-speed car accidents. Here's what a typical test day is like for one of these humanlike machines.

1. The Checkup

A technician examines the dummy to make sure the sensors inside it work and its neck and joints move like a real person's would.

2. Strapping In

Workers load the dummy into the car in a realistic position. They take measurements to ensure that it's sitting in exactly the right spot.

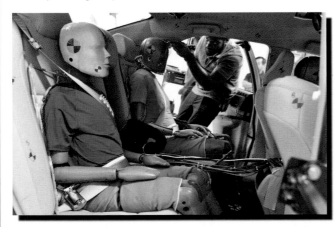

3. Wild Ride

When all systems are go, the engineers start the car moving. The dummy's sensors start recording as the car speeds up, moves forward, and slams into the wall.

4. First Report

As soon as the test is over, the dummy starts sending data to the engineers wirelessly. It tells them which parts of its body sustained forces that would injure a real person.

5. Take a Break

Technicians photograph the dummy in the car, then bring it back to the lab to check all its parts and sensors. The dummy's job is done—that is, until the next scheduled crash!

DUMMIES COME IN DIFFERENT SHAPES AND BODY SIZES TO SIMULATE **ADULT MEN AND WOMEN** OF DIFFERENT AGES AND **CHILDREN.**

SHOCK ABSORBER

How do self-destructing **FUSES** prevent electrical meltdowns?

Electricity is a glorious thing. It lets us charge our screens, refrigerate our food, and keep the lights on after the sun goes down. But electricity can be extremely dangerous, which is why many machines and high-voltage power lines come equipped with electrical fuses. These humble devices sacrifice themselves to protect us if there's a potentially perilous power surge. What are power surges, and how do fuses stop them from destroying homes and electric power grids? Get charged up, because we're about to find out.

What are fuses for **?**

What are they made of **?**

How do they help prevent fires **?**

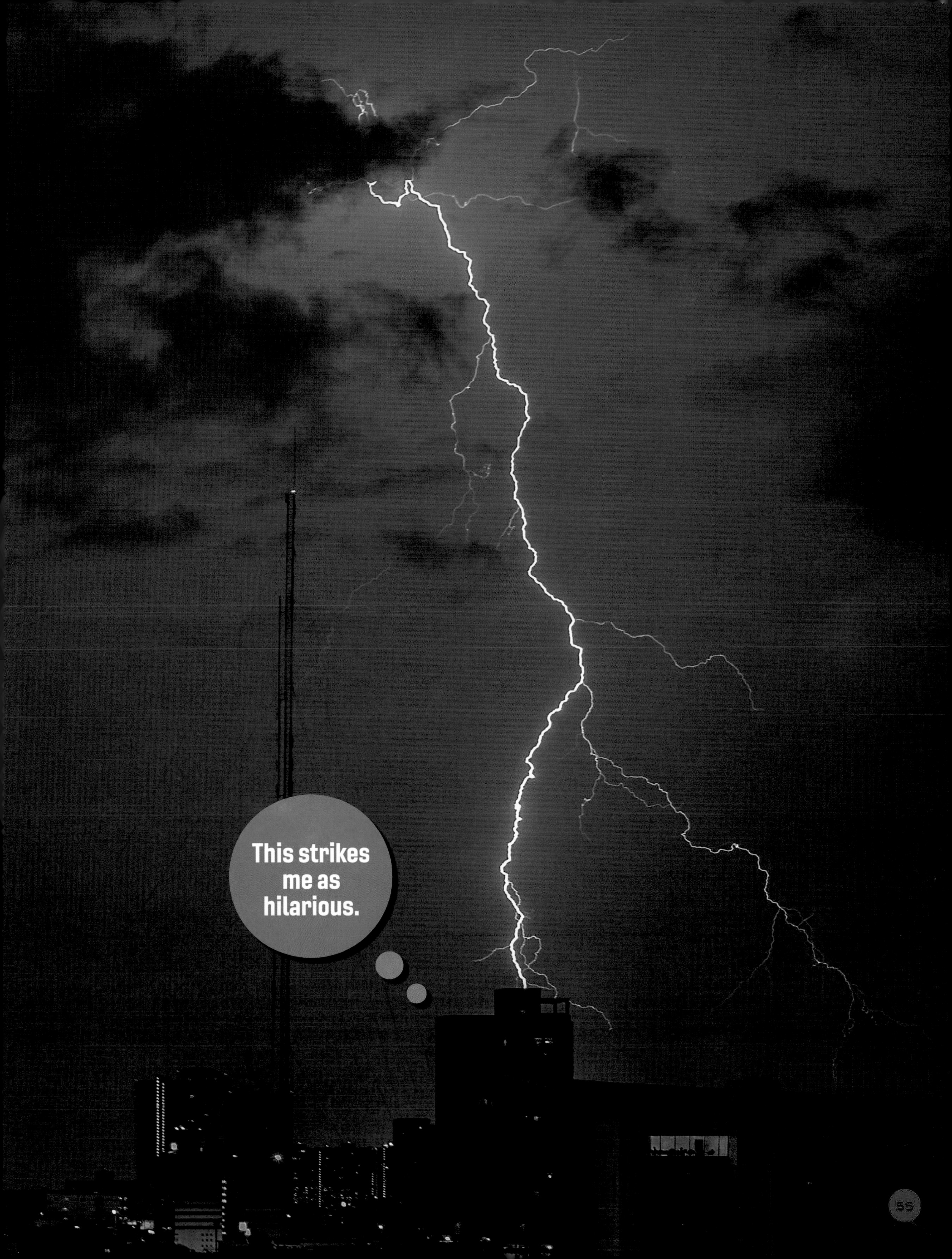
This strikes me as hilarious.

JUST THE FACTS

Electric Overload

Electricity is complicated stuff, but it's basically moving electrons—tiny particles that bounce from atom to atom inside a material, carrying electrical charge with them. This charge provides the energy to start a car or switch on a television (to name two of millions of examples). But if too much electricity flows into a device, parts of it can fizzle, catch fire, or even explode. That's where our friend the fuse comes in.

In the Loop

Electricity needs to move in a circuit—an unbroken loop of materials that electrons can flow through. Fuses are designed to be part of this circuit, whether they're inside an appliance like a refrigerator or on top of a neighborhood power line (where they're the twisty-looking cylinders holding a long, thin tube). But the fuse is the weakest, easiest-to-destroy part of the circuit. And that's on purpose. If more electricity starts flowing through a system than it can safely carry—because there's a lightning strike, say, or the wiring is damaged—the fuse melts away. This breaks the loop, stopping the flow of electricity in the circuit and protecting everything connected to it from dangerous overload.

INSIDE A FUSE

Fuses come in different shapes and sizes depending on what they're protecting. But the basic design is always the same. Take a look at how one type works.

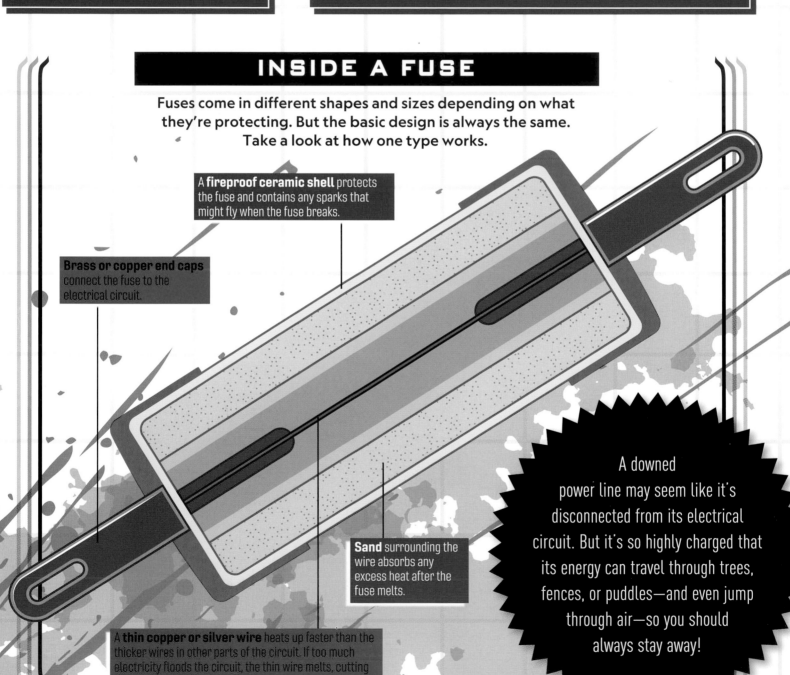

A **fireproof ceramic shell** protects the fuse and contains any sparks that might fly when the fuse breaks.

Brass or copper end caps connect the fuse to the electrical circuit.

Sand surrounding the wire absorbs any excess heat after the fuse melts.

A **thin copper or silver wire** heats up faster than the thicker wires in other parts of the circuit. If too much electricity floods the circuit, the thin wire melts, cutting off the current's flow.

A downed power line may seem like it's disconnected from its electrical circuit. But it's so highly charged that its energy can travel through trees, fences, or puddles—and even jump through air—so you should always stay away!

TELL ME MORE

THE WEAKEST LINK

So, hold up—why does a thinner wire melt faster than a thicker metal end cap in an electrical surge? It comes down to something called electrical resistance, or how hard it is for electricity to flow. As electrons move through a wire, they heat up the wire. But the thinner a wire is, the harder it is for the electrons to move through it, and the more heat it creates. (This property is put to good use in a toaster, where the wires are just thin enough to force the moving electrons to warm up your toast.) The thin wire of the fuse heats up faster than the end caps, melting the fuse before the rest of the copper in the circuit even gets very warm.

FUN FACTS

>>> Some of the first **ELECTRICAL FUSES** were used in the mid-1800s to protect **TELEGRAPH** stations from **LIGHTNING** strikes.

>>> A thin fuse just a **FEW INCHES** long can protect a **MILE** of thicker wire.

>>> If the **HEAT OVERLOAD** on a fuse is big enough, the **SAND INSIDE IT MELTS** into solid glassy clumps!

This fuse keeps the circuit safe.

WHOA... SLOW DOWN. A CLOSER LOOK AT CIRCUITS.

Let's loop back and talk about why electricity moves in a circuit. Electrons are usually orbiting quickly around atoms, the tiny particles that make up, well, everything. In some materials, such as copper, an electron can easily bounce away from its home atom and move to the one next door. When it does, it leaves an opening for another electron to jump into. Many electrons moving down a line of atoms in the same direction creates an electrical flow. But in order for the flow to keep going, every moving electron needs a new atom in front of it to bounce into—which is why the circuit has to make a loop and connect back to where it started. When you plug in an electrical device, it becomes part of that circuit: Electrons flow in through one side of the cord, move through the device to operate it, then flow back into the wall on the other side. That's why plugs have two prongs—in one end and out the other!

BIG BANGS

How do **FIREWORKS** destroy themselves to make a dazzling light show?

Boom! Pow! Oh, wow! Big, bright, colorful, and noisy, fireworks are signs of celebration around the world. From classic flowery bursts to sparkling shapes like hearts, stars, and smiley faces, they're a surefire way to wow a crowd. But how do these colorful explosions light up the night? It's a spectacular act of self-destruction, so check it out—it might blow your mind.

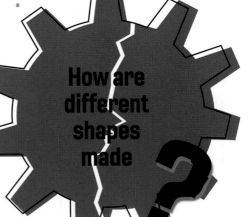

What are fireworks made of ?

How do they launch into the sky ?

How are different shapes made ?

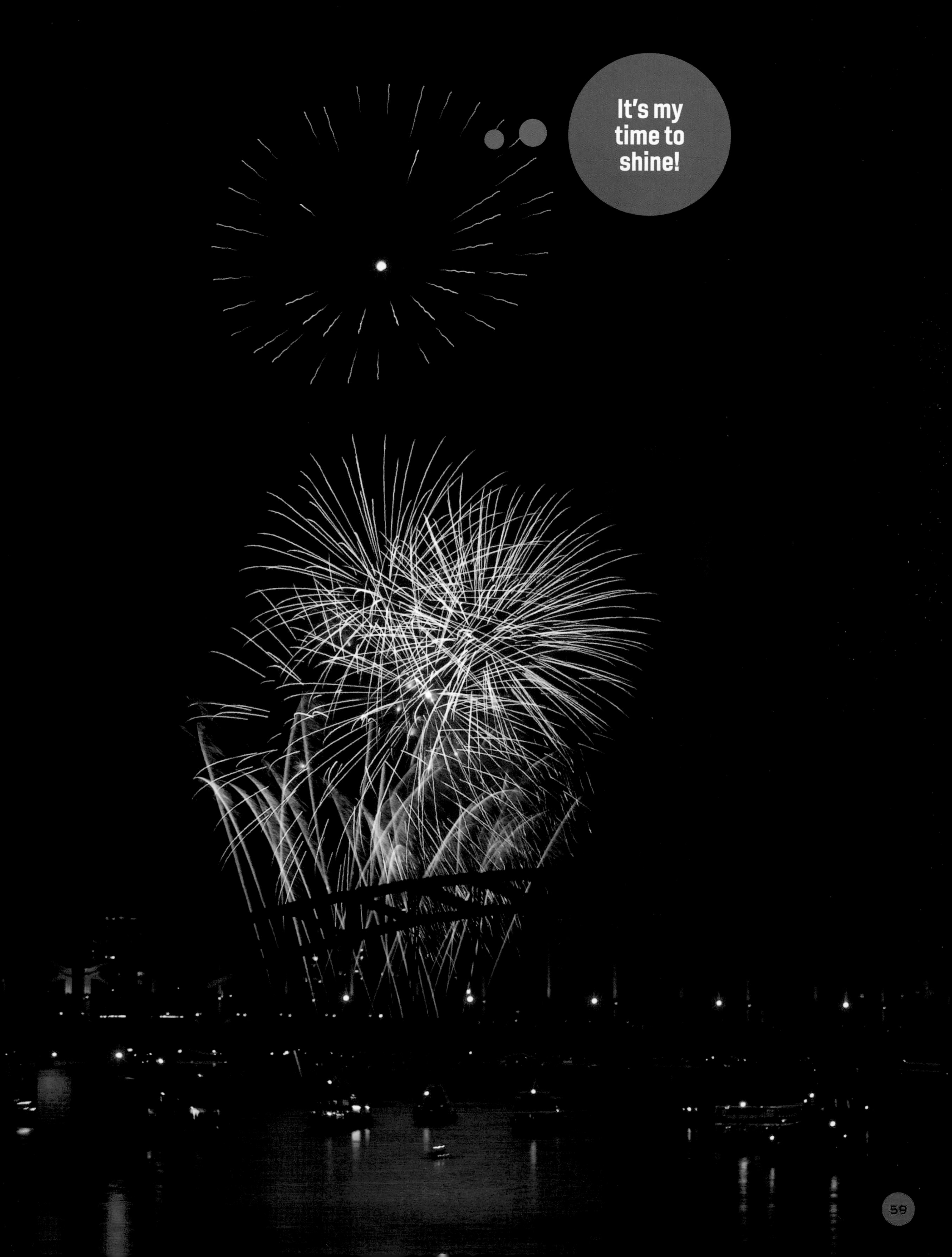
It's my time to shine!

JUST THE FACTS

It's a Blast

Fireworks come in many shapes and sizes, but we're going to talk about the big ones: the sky-high bursts controlled by professional pyrotechnicians (aka explosives operators) at holiday celebrations and special events. These are known as aerial fireworks, and the people designing the show pick from dozens of colors and patterns. They combine everything from slow sparkly drifters to giant spectacular starbursts into a phenomenal light show.

Cool Chemistry

As magical as it looks, the basic construction of a firework is pretty simple. It's kind of like an explosive piñata in a layered paper shell. Inside the shell is explosive black powder, along with "stars" that contain metals such as aluminum, iron, and magnesium. When the shell catches fire, these metallic compounds explode outward and burn hot enough to glow in different colors depending on what they're made of.

STELLAR SHAPES

Fireworks come in a dazzling array of shapes and colors.
How many of these have you seen?

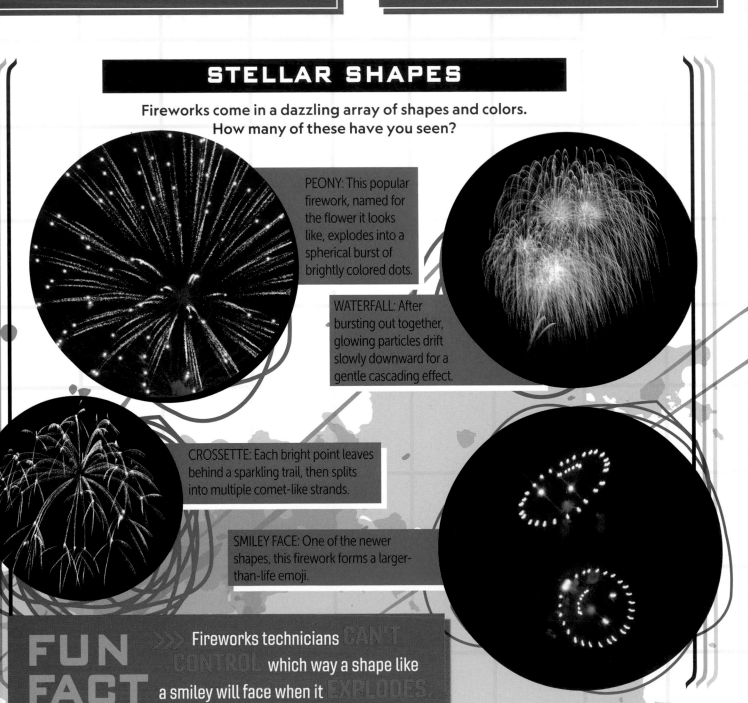

PEONY: This popular firework, named for the flower it looks like, explodes into a spherical burst of brightly colored dots.

WATERFALL: After bursting out together, glowing particles drift slowly downward for a gentle cascading effect.

CROSSETTE: Each bright point leaves behind a sparkling trail, then splits into multiple comet-like strands.

SMILEY FACE: One of the newer shapes, this firework forms a larger-than-life emoji.

FUN FACT >>> Fireworks technicians CAN'T CONTROL which way a shape like a smiley will face when it EXPLODES.

INSIDE A FIREWORK

A firework's shell is packed with explosives and chemical pellets called stars.
These need to burn in the right order for a beautiful burst of light.

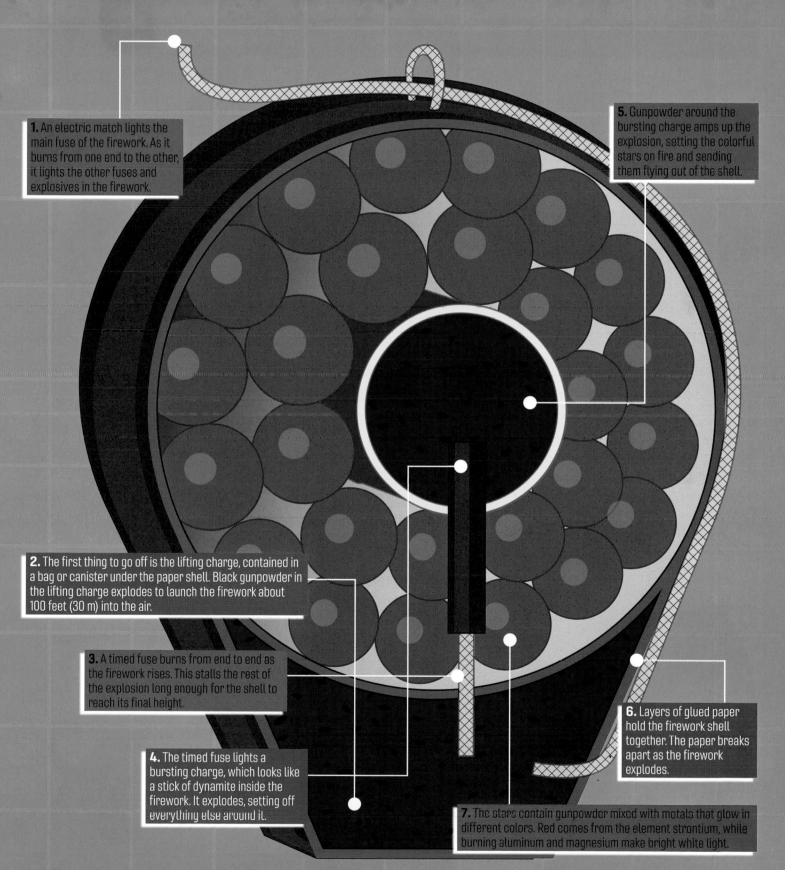

1. An electric match lights the main fuse of the firework. As it burns from one end to the other, it lights the other fuses and explosives in the firework.

5. Gunpowder around the bursting charge amps up the explosion, setting the colorful stars on fire and sending them flying out of the shell.

2. The first thing to go off is the lifting charge, contained in a bag or canister under the paper shell. Black gunpowder in the lifting charge explodes to launch the firework about 100 feet (30 m) into the air.

3. A timed fuse burns from end to end as the firework rises. This stalls the rest of the explosion long enough for the shell to reach its final height.

6. Layers of glued paper hold the firework shell together. The paper breaks apart as the firework explodes.

4. The timed fuse lights a bursting charge, which looks like a stick of dynamite inside the firework. It explodes, setting off everything else around it.

7. The stars contain gunpowder mixed with metals that glow in different colors. Red comes from the element strontium, while burning aluminum and magnesium make bright white light.

TELL ME MORE

THE ART OF EXPLOSION

Crafting an awe-inspiring fireworks display takes creativity and precision. But pyrotechnicians can't practice a performance without wasting a *lot* of expensive fireworks. Instead, they sketch what they want a show to look like, then simulate it on computers. They pick different colors, sizes, and shapes of fireworks to create the effects they want and decide what order they should fire in. Then they arrange each shell in a tube-shaped mortar connected to an electric "match" that will set it off. They can control where a firework ends up in the sky by adjusting the angle of the mortar (like aiming a cannon). Each electric match is wired to a computer system that tells it when to fire. This allows the pyrotechnicians to stay a safe distance away from the explosions. After months of preparation, they just press a button and wait for the blast to begin.

FUN FACTS

>>> Machines now help with many parts of a **FIREWORKS SHOW.** but packing stars into shells is still done carefully **BY HAND.**

>>> The biggest ever **AERIAL FIREWORK** was launched in **STEAMBOAT SPRINGS,** Colorado, U.S.A., in 2020. The supersized shell measured **4 FEET 8 INCHES** (1.4 m) across and exploded into 380 individual comet-shaped bursts.

>>> A **NEW YEAR'S** celebration in 2016 in the Philippines set a world record for the **LARGEST FIREWORKS** display. The show started at midnight and ended **810,904 FIREWORKS** later— just after 1 a.m.!

The dazzling 2016 fireworks display in the Philippines

A massive firework goes off over Steamboat Springs, Colorado.

PACKING A PRETTY PUNCH

The size and arrangement of stars inside a shell, as well as what it's made of, affect how a firework looks when it explodes.

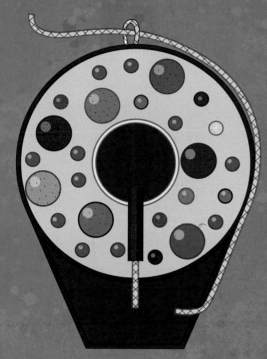

MIXING colored stars creates multicolored fireworks. Bigger stars burn brighter or for longer than smaller ones.

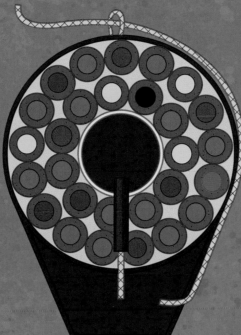

STARS layered with different **metal compounds** change color as they're burning. The outside color shows up first, followed by the inside color as the star smolders away.

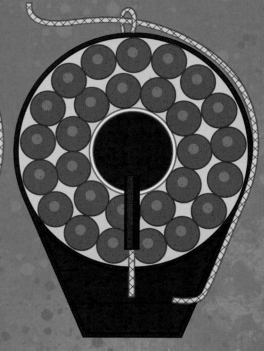

STARS can be packed randomly or arranged to explode into a particular pattern. Here, each line of colored stars will be pushed outward into a ring.

HOW THINGS WORKED

We may associate fireworks with modern holidays, but they date back millennia. The first ones are thought to have been developed in China around 200 B.C. Back then, people roasted hollow stalks of bamboo over an open fire. Pockets of air inside the bamboo expanded as they heated up, finally bursting with a loud CRACK. About a thousand years later, Chinese alchemists discovered how to make gunpowder. It didn't take long for people to realize that packing it into bamboo firecrackers made for bigger and more satisfying bursts. To add some sparkle, they shaved bits of iron off old pots and pans and mixed them with the gunpowder. The shavings gave off a golden glow when heated—which they're still used for in some fireworks today. People in China haven't forgotten this explosive history. *Baozhu,* the Mandarin word for firecracker, literally translates to "exploding bamboo"!

Bamboo roasting over a fire

LESSON LEARNED!
FIREWORKS FAIL
JULY 4, 2012

The Incident

On July 4, 2012, half a million people crowded into parks and beaches in San Diego, California, to watch the Independence Day fireworks. Four barges in the San Diego Bay were packed with thousands of explosive shells. Organizers had promised a larger spectacle than ever before. And they delivered—but not in the way they had planned.

At 8:55 p.m., the show's operator pressed a button to start the fireworks. The sky erupted in towering fireballs of white, yellow, and orange light. Booms filled the air, and the crowd oohed and aahed—but only for about 30 seconds. Then they looked around in confusion as the show suddenly ended.

Everyone quickly realized what had happened. Instead of going off in sequence over the course of 17 minutes, all 7,000 fireworks had exploded at the same time! Luckily, no one was hurt in the incident. But a few people who'd paid for prime viewing spots did ask for refunds.

What Went Wrong

After apologizing to the disappointed crowds, the fireworks company investigated the accident. Nothing like this had happened at its shows before. Plus, workers had tested every component they could in the weeks before the failed display. What could possibly have gone wrong? The culprit turned out to be the computers running the show. These automated systems control the timing and lighting of each firework so workers can stay a safe distance away. But the fireworks company accidentally combined two files as they were loaded onto the computers before the show. That created a glitch that told the computers to launch all the fireworks at once.

THE BIG TAKEAWAY

RUNNING A FIREWORKS SHOW IS EXTREMELY COMPLICATED. Organizers plan carefully and have many safety precautions in place. They test the files that run the program before the event. But they can't practice launching the fireworks, or there'd be nothing left to use in the show. Sometimes the only way to discover a problem is to experience it—and once you know it can happen, you figure out how to keep it from happening again. The company that blew it in San Diego learned from its experience. It offered to run the city's fireworks for free the next year, and everything went off without a hitch.

WHEN NO ONE GETS HURT, FIREWORKS FAILURES CAN BE FUNNY. **MILLIONS** OF PEOPLE AROUND THE WORLD WATCHED VIDEOS OF THE **DISASTROUS SAN DIEGO DISPLAY.** BUT **MANY ACCIDENTS** SERIOUSLY HURT AND KILL PEOPLE.

Fireworks that launch in unexpected directions start tens of thousands of fires every year. That's why it's important to always follow the law. Kids and amateurs should never handle fireworks. Trained professionals—like these individuals in Edinburgh, Scotland—should always run the show. They know how to prepare and inspect each and every firework.

Fireworks technicians go through careful checklists before, during, and after a fireworks show—and they work with local fire departments and medical providers to make sure everyone is ready in case of an emergency.

HEAD PROTECTOR

How do **PLASTIC AND FOAM** protect your brain in a bike crash?

Falling off your bike is painful. You might bruise your arm, skin your knee, or even slam your head on the ground. But if you have any brains, you should protect them by wearing a helmet, which is designed to absorb the nastier forces of a bike crash. Let's learn more about how helmets keep your noggin safe—but try not to lose your head over it, OK?

What are bike helmets made of **?**

Why do we need them **?**

How can helmet design get even better **?**

JUST THE FACTS

Crash Pad

A helmet doesn't just keep your head from scraping the sidewalk. Its main job is to absorb energy from a crash so your soft, squishy brain doesn't have to. If you crash your bike, your body is probably moving fast. A helmet is designed to crack and compress when it hits the pavement to help your brain slow down more gently. If your brain bounces around too hard inside your skull, you could suffer a serious brain injury called a concussion.

Juuust Right

One of the most important things about a helmet's design is the material. It can't be too weak or too strong. If the helmet were too sturdy, it would be no better than hitting your head on the pavement. Too delicate, and it could break apart immediately, leaving your poor head to take most of the hit. A light-but-firm material called expanded polystyrene foam is the perfect compromise. It contains thousands of tiny air bubbles between thin walls of plastic. When it hits the ground, the foam presses together, absorbing energy from the crash.

MAJOR IMPACT

Here's how a head-on impact can cause a concussion—and how a helmet can stop one.

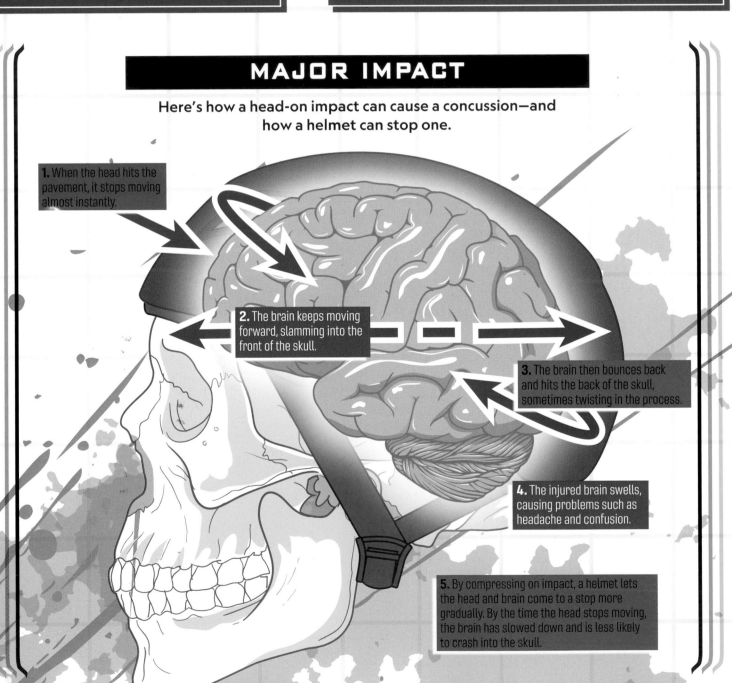

1. When the head hits the pavement, it stops moving almost instantly.

2. The brain keeps moving forward, slamming into the front of the skull.

3. The brain then bounces back and hits the back of the skull, sometimes twisting in the process.

4. The injured brain swells, causing problems such as headache and confusion.

5. By compressing on impact, a helmet lets the head and brain come to a stop more gradually. By the time the head stops moving, the brain has slowed down and is less likely to crash into the skull.

TELL ME MORE

MIND YOUR MOTION

Your brain is made of a jellylike material. It's surrounded by a layer of fluid inside your bony skull. The fluid protects your brain from bumping against your skull as you go about your day. But what if your head changes speed too quickly—say, because it falls and hits the sidewalk, going from moving quickly to stopping completely? Then the fluid isn't enough to absorb the force of the crash. Inertia (the tendency of a moving object to stay in motion) keeps your brain traveling in the same direction your head was going, and at the same speed. It slams against the inside of your skull, potentially causing a concussion.

FUN FACTS

>>> The **EXPANDED POLYSTYRENE** in a helmet is more than **95 PERCENT AIR!**

>>> One way engineers test a helmet is to put it on a **DUMMY HEAD** and drop it onto an anvil.

INSIDE A HELMET

The Multidirectional Impact Protection System (MIPS) adds an extra layer of protection to the safety features of a typical bike helmet. Here's how the layers work together to reduce the forces of a crash.

A **thin outer shell** made of lightweight plastic protects the material underneath from minor bumps and scrapes.

A **thick layer of expanded polystyrene foam** squishes under pressure, reducing the force of an impact.

A **MIPS layer** attached by rubber straps slides separately from the outer shell. This lets the helmet rotate slightly as it hits the ground, absorbing any twisting forces before they reach the brain.

Some helmets include an **adjustable visor** that shields you from sun, rain, and branches—and offers some protection for your face in case of a crash.

WHOA...SLOW DOWN. A CLOSER LOOK AT INERTIA.

Inertia is a fundamental rule of physics: A moving object will keep moving unless an outside force stops it. Sometimes inertia can be helpful: If you're riding along a flat path and take a break from pedaling, your bike's inertia is what keeps it coasting (until the wheels dragging against the ground slow it down). But the bike isn't the only thing moving forward—so is anything on the bike, like your body. If the bike stops suddenly, your body's inertia can throw you over the handlebars. And if your head hits the ground, your brain's inertia throws it against your skull.

BURN, BABY, BURN

How does a self-destructing **SPACECRAFT** protect astronauts?

Imagine you're an astronaut. Your mission completed, you're in a capsule plummeting back toward Earth. Your body shakes in your seat as you fall at thousands of miles an hour. Out the window, you see hot, bright flames pouring over the sides of the spacecraft. But you know you're safe despite the alarming view. How? It's all about the spacecraft's heat shield. Check it out in t-minus 5, 4, 3, 2, 1…

Why is returning from space so dangerous **?**

How do heat shields keep spacecraft from burning up **?**

What will heat shields of the future look like **?**

JUST THE FACTS

Hot, Hot Heat

There are plenty of perils involved in space travel, beginning with blasting off while sitting atop a tank of explosive rocket fuel. But, in fact, one of the most dangerous parts of going to space is coming back. A spacecraft has to move fast to launch into Earth's orbit, and slowing down before coming home would take more fuel than is practical. Instead, a reentry capsule plummets back into Earth's atmosphere, rubbing against millions of air molecules on the way down. This rubbing creates friction that helps slow the spacecraft, but can also heat it to nearly 3000 degrees Fahrenheit (1600°C)—hotter than the inside of a volcano. That's hot enough to melt most materials in a spacecraft, not to mention the astronauts inside. Protecting them is a major challenge.

Soaking It Up

Have you ever heard the phrase "take the heat"? It's basically a heat shield's motto. The shield's job is to absorb—and be destroyed by—heat, so nothing else is damaged. Scientists and engineers have devised a few ingenious ways to build these superpowered shields. One is layering heat-absorbing tiles on the side of the spacecraft that hits the atmosphere. Another method is coating a reentry capsule with plastic resin that burns up as it hurtles through the atmosphere. It might sound scary to have part of your spaceship burn up, but better that than the capsule itself, right?

BLAZE OF GLORY

Earth's atmosphere burns up anything that falls into it unprotected. Meteors—aka shooting stars—are space rocks hitting this floating force field. Friction from all the air molecules incinerates them on their way down.

SPARKLING SKY: Every August, meteors light up the sky in the Northern Hemisphere as Earth passes through the trail of debris from a comet. The particles are generally no bigger than a marble, but the bright flashes as they burn up in Earth's atmosphere can be seen from the ground.

SHOT FROM SPACE: On October 9, 1992, a sparkling space rock blazed through the sky in Peekskill, New York, U.S.A., startling fans at a local football game. One burning chunk that survived the trip to Earth smashed right through the tail of a teenager's car.

GREAT BALL OF FIRE: On the morning of February 15, 2013, a space rock the size of a six-story building broke up over Chelyabinsk, Russia. Witnesses saw a fireball about as bright as the sun make an arc for 300 miles (480 km), and scientists later fished a 1,260-pound (570-kg) piece of the rock out of a nearby lake.

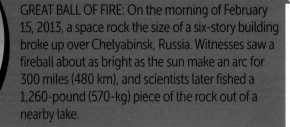

BURNING OFF

An ablative heat shield is designed to sizzle away as it enters Earth's atmosphere. Here's how it worked on the capsule that brought astronauts home from the moon.

Fiberglass formed into a honeycomb pattern gave the heat shield its structure. Each cell of the honeycomb was filled with plastic resin that went in as liquid, then hardened like glue.

The wide, curved face of the shield acted like an umbrella for oncoming air particles, steering them around the edges of the capsule. Less air hitting the sides and back of the spacecraft meant less friction on those parts.

As the resin burned up, it became hot gas. The gas floated away from the spacecraft, carrying dangerous heat away too.

Air molecules pounding the front and edges of the shield heated up the resin, which started to char. From the ground, it looked like the whole capsule was on fire.

FUN FACT >>> Spacecraft reenter EARTH'S ATMOSPHERE at around 17,500 MILES AN HOUR (28,200 km/h)—more than 20 times faster than the SPEED OF SOUND.

According to the laws of physics, the bigger an object coming in for a landing, the more heat it generates. And that doesn't just go for entering Earth's atmosphere—it's true for landing on Mars too. Mars's atmosphere is only about one-hundredth the thickness of Earth's, but it still creates plenty of friction. And when space explorers eventually make their way to the planet, they'll need to bring up to 20 tons (18 t) of scientific equipment and survival supplies. A traditional heat shield for all this stuff would have to be enormous—and enormously heavy. Enter the Hypersonic Inflatable Aerodynamic Decelerator, or HIAD. NASA is developing this lightweight, inflatable heat shield in the hopes that the agency can use it to deliver heavy equipment to Mars.

FUN FACT

»»» NASA engineers have developed a HEAT SHIELD so effective it can keep scientific instruments NEAR ROOM TEMPERATURE as the spacecraft they're on approaches the EDGE OF THE SUN.

Protective tiles from the space shuttle *Columbia*

HOW THINGS WORKED

From 1981 to 2011, the U.S. launched astronauts in reusable space shuttles. Instead of a heat shield that would have to be replaced each time, the shuttles were covered with more than 21,000 heat-absorbing tiles. But some engineers had concerns about how well the tiles stuck on when the shuttle blasted off and landed. In fact, this proved to be a deadly problem on a 2003 mission. When the shuttle *Columbia* launched that year, a 1.7-pound (0.77-kg) piece of foam broke off from the fuel tank and hit one of the shuttle's wings. No one was sure if it had caused serious damage. But when the spacecraft came back from orbit 16 days later, it broke apart in Earth's atmosphere, killing all seven astronauts on board. An investigation found that the flying foam had punched a hole in one of the wing's protective tiles. This let superhot air leak into the shuttle during reentry, destroying the spacecraft. The shuttle fleet was grounded for two years while NASA redesigned the fuel tank. Engineers also developed a repair kit that future astronauts could use in orbit to prevent the same tragedy from happening again.

POCKET PROTECTOR

Unlike other heat shields, the HIAD would fold to take up less space on the nine-month journey to the red planet. Then it would pop open to slow the lander and protect it from the heat of entering the atmosphere.

The lander separates from the spacecraft.

As the lander enters Mars's atmosphere, an inflation device pumps air into the folded-up HIAD, spreading it into a cone shape.

Fabric woven with a gritty material called silicon carbide protects the outside of the inflated device. The high-tech heat-resistant fabric steers hot gas away from the rest of the lander without burning up.

Scientific instruments and other supplies are protected from the intense heat that friction with the atmosphere generates.

The doughnut-shaped tubes that hold the air are made of tough braided fibers like Kevlar. When woven together, the material is 15 times stronger than steel.

TRY THIS!

SNACK SMASHER

BUILD A PACKAGE TO PROTECT A PRECIOUS TREAT

When a package arrives at your doorstep, you may not think of it as a marvel of engineering. But there are people whose entire job consists of designing packaging to protect products on their way to your home. All that cardboard, tape, and bubble wrap are organized carefully to absorb the force from any bumps on the journey. The box can get a bit beat up, as long as the stuff inside it remains safe. Can you build a package that absorbs enough force to protect a snack inside?

WHAT YOU NEED

TIME: About an hour

1. An adult to supervise and help with cutting

2. One large individually wrapped breakable snack item (think hard pretzels, chips, or crunchy granola bars)

3. Pencil and paper

4. Cardboard box from the recycling bin

5. Scissors

6. Tape

7. Other packaging materials, such as bubble wrap, foam padding, crumpled paper, and egg cartons

1. Study the snack and the packaging it has already. How is it designed to protect the food inside?

2. Think about how you could use the cardboard and other materials to package the snack so it won't be damaged when you drop, throw, and kick it. Sketch your plan on the paper.

3. Ask an adult to help cut and fold the cardboard into the shape you want. Arrange the snack and your other packaging materials according to your plan. Seal the outside with tape.

4. With an adult's supervision, take the package outside. Then beat it up! Throw and kick the package around. Slam it to the ground.

5. After a few minutes of beating up the package, carefully open it and inspect the snack. How did it hold up?

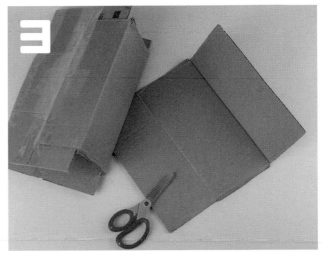

CAUTION:

Before eating it, be sure your snack's packaging hasn't been damaged or opened. Always check with an adult to be safe.

cardboard

CHIPS

tape

Paper

WHAT TO EXPECT

THE FATE OF YOUR FOOD DEPENDS ON HOW WELL YOU DESIGNED YOUR PACKAGE. A SUCCESSFUL DESIGN WILL KEEP THE SNACK IN ONE PIECE. IF THE TREAT COMES OUT CRUMBLED OR CRUSHED WITHIN ITS WRAPPER, YOUR DESIGN NEEDS ADJUSTING. THINK ABOUT WHAT CHANGES YOU COULD MAKE.

WHAT'S GOING ON?

CAR BODIES AND BIKE HELMETS CHANGE SHAPE TO ABSORB THE FORCE OF AN IMPACT. THAT'S WHAT YOUR PACKAGING HAS TO DO TO KEEP THE FORCE OF YOUR THROWS AND KICKS FROM TRANSFERRING TO THE SNACK INSIDE. BUT IT CAN'T CHANGE SHAPE TOO MUCH, OR IT MIGHT BREAK ALL THE WAY OPEN. THAT WOULD LEAVE YOUR PRECIOUS CARGO WITH NO PROTECTION.

CHAPTER 3
FAMOUS FAILURES

The Great Pyramid of Giza.
The Taj Mahal. The Eiffel Tower.
PEOPLE OF THE PAST HAVE CONSTRUCTED SOME AWE-INSPIRING STRUCTURES.

But that's obviously not what we're here for. How about some of the most spectacularly disastrous engineering failures of all time? Let's explore how bridges buckled, towers teetered, pyramids bent, and an exploding tank of sweetener terrorized a city. The bright side? Scientists and engineers are still learning from these catastrophes to build things better and stronger today.

THE TITANIC

Was the *Titanic*'s fate UNAVOIDABLE— or did design flaws spell its doom?

The night of April 14, 1912, has never been forgotten. That's when an iceberg sank the British passenger liner *Titanic,* killing most people aboard. For more than a century since, people have argued about what happened. Did the engineers build the ship wrong? Was the captain driving recklessly? Was it just a tragic accident that couldn't have been avoided? We're about to go deep into the *Titanic*'s design to find out what brought the ship down. Make sure you've got your life jacket on.

What keeps a giant ship afloat?

How did the iceberg damage the *Titanic*?

Was the ship's design at fault?

JUST THE FACTS

Unlucky Launch

On April 10, 1912, the *Titanic* departed England for the first time, headed for New York City. On board were about 900 crew members and 1,300 passengers. For months, newspapers had hailed the *Titanic* as one of the finest ships ever built—they even called it "unsinkable." But disaster struck four days into the voyage in an icy area of the Atlantic. At 11:40 p.m. on April 14, a lookout spotted an iceberg straight ahead of the ship. The first officer frantically tried turning the ship to avoid it, but it was too late. The side of the *Titanic* scraped against the roughly 300-foot (90-m)-long iceberg, which pierced the steel hull. Over the next two and a half hours, the ship flooded with water, finally sinking. Famously, there weren't enough lifeboats to save everyone aboard—which is part of why more than 1,500 people lost their lives. But there were deeper problems with the ship's design that also helped seal its fate.

Staying Afloat

It may seem mind-boggling that a skyscraper-size ship like the *Titanic* floated in the first place. But the secret is density—how much something weighs compared to its size. To float, an object has to weigh less than an equal-size volume of water (in other words, to be less dense than the water). A ship like the *Titanic* contains thousands of tons of heavy metal, which is denser than water. If you crumpled the whole thing into a ball, it would sink like a rock. But such a spacious ship also contains a lot of air—which weighs almost nothing. This makes the ship less dense than water on average, so it stays afloat. That's all well and good until an iceberg scrapes the hull open. Then water flows in, replacing the air inside the ship and weighing it down, making it sink.

WORLD'S FINEST SHIP?

Before sinking, the *Titanic* was considered a technical marvel for its day. Here are a few of the luxurious and innovative features that made its passengers especially excited to board.

The *Titanic* was powered by two steam engines that were the largest of their kind ever built at the time. Each one was more than three stories tall and weighed about 1,000 tons (900 t).

An intricate grand staircase spiraled down five decks of the first-class area. Wealthy passengers could also make use of an onboard swimming pool, squash court, and spa.

The ship had one of the first wireless telegraph systems that could transmit a signal through open air. This helped the crew send distress signals to nearby ships.

The *Titanic*'s first-class passengers used some of the earliest onboard elevators to carry them between decks of the ship—complete with couches to sit on while they enjoyed the ride.

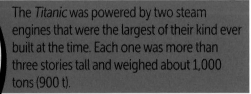

BUILDING BIG

Despite its massive size, the *Titanic* could float because of all the air it contained—as well as a few key elements of the ship's design

Most of the space in the passenger compartments was air. This kept the average density of the ship light enough to float despite its weight.

Heavy tanks in the base of the ship held up to 5,754 tons (5,220 t) of water. This water powered the steam engines and served as ballast—meaning the tanks could be filled or emptied to help balance the ship.

The wide shape of the ship's hull helped it displace, or push aside, water. The water pushed back up against the ship, creating buoyancy that kept it afloat.

With its metal hull fully loaded with passengers, crew, supplies, and cargo, the *Titanic* weighed about 52,300 tons (47,400 t).

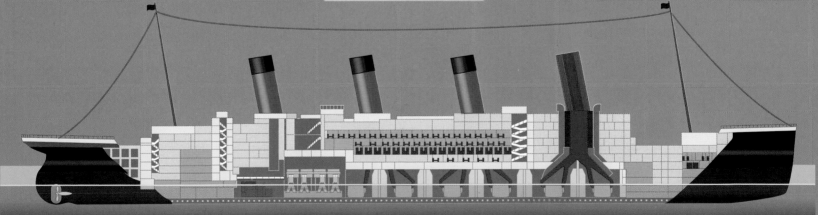

FUN FACT >>> Binoculars might have helped the ship's LOOKOUTS spot the ICEBERG sooner. But they weren't using them because NO ONE KNEW where on the ship they'd been stored.

TELL ME MORE

SEALING THE SHIP'S FATE

Any ship worth its salt has built-in ways to keep floating even if its hull is damaged. The *Titanic* was no different—or so its designers thought. The ship's hull was divided into 16 compartments separated by steel walls called bulkheads. The bulkheads had watertight doors at the bottom. In an emergency, the crew could flip a switch to swing these doors shut to keep the water contained. According to the shipbuilders' calculations, four of the compartments could fill with water and the ship could still make it safely to port—it was "unsinkable," remember? But the bulkheads didn't go all the way to the deck above, so water could spill over the top. When the ship scraped the iceberg, six of the hull compartments were torn open. And as the front of the ship took on seawater and tipped downward, water poured over the walls from one "watertight" compartment into the next.

>>> Milton Hershey, who created the Hershey **CHOCOLATE BAR,** was planning to travel home from vacation on the *Titanic*. But a business meeting **CALLED HIM BACK** sooner, and he missed the fateful trip.

>>> A **NEARBY SHIP** may have been able to rescue more *Titanic* passengers, but the crew **DIDN'T HEAR** its distress calls because they'd **TURNED OFF** the radio for the night. Ships are now required to keep their radios on **AROUND THE CLOCK.**

>>> Talk about **UNLUCKY:** One of the *Titanic*'s sister ships, the *Britannic*, capsized after hitting a **MINE** during World War I. A nurse who survived that 1916 incident was also on the *Titanic*—but **ESCAPED THAT TOO.**

The *Britannic*

TRY THIS!

How did water spilling over walls inside the ship make it sink? Try it out for yourself with your own mini-hull. Grab an ice cube tray and a bowl or pan large enough to hold it. Fill the container with enough water to float your ice cube tray. Pour a few spoonfuls of water into the front few compartments, and it should stay up. But then tip the front corner into the water so the compartments can keep filling and the water pours over the dividers. The tray should start to sink.

HOW SHE SANK

In the two and a half hours after the *Titanic* struck an iceberg, problems piled up that overwhelmed the ship's design.

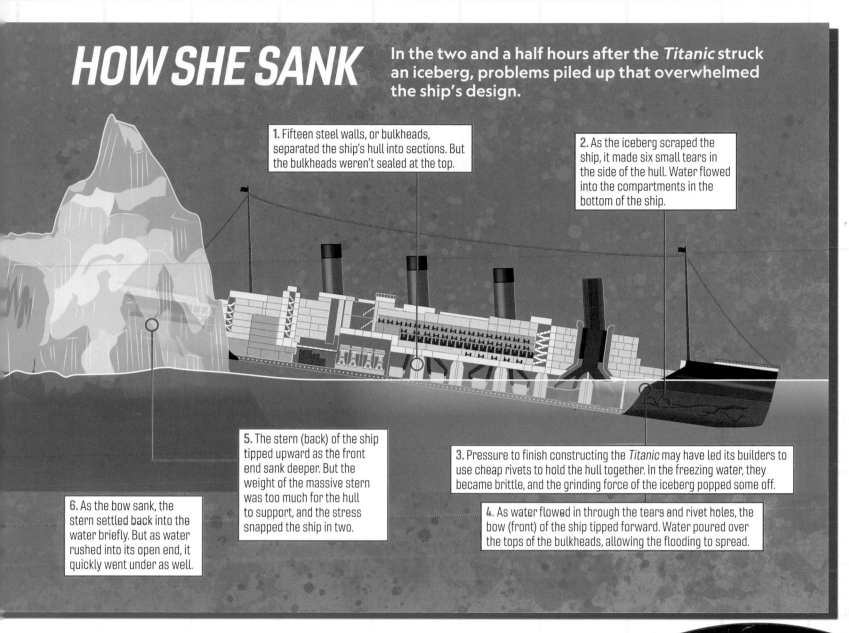

1. Fifteen steel walls, or bulkheads, separated the ship's hull into sections. But the bulkheads weren't sealed at the top.

2. As the iceberg scraped the ship, it made six small tears in the side of the hull. Water flowed into the compartments in the bottom of the ship.

5. The stern (back) of the ship tipped upward as the front end sank deeper. But the weight of the massive stern was too much for the hull to support, and the stress snapped the ship in two.

3. Pressure to finish constructing the *Titanic* may have led its builders to use cheap rivets to hold the hull together. In the freezing water, they became brittle, and the grinding force of the iceberg popped some off.

6. As the bow sank, the stern settled back into the water briefly. But as water rushed into its open end, it quickly went under as well.

4. As water flowed in through the tears and rivet holes, the bow (front) of the ship tipped forward. Water poured over the tops of the bulkheads, allowing the flooding to spread.

MYTH VERSUS FACT

As soon as news spread of the *Titanic*'s sinking, people tried to guess what had happened. The U.S. and Great Britain launched investigations. Interviews with surviving passengers and crew helped authorities piece events together, but with the remains of the ship lost 13,000 feet (4,000 m) deep in the Atlantic, there was a lot of guesswork. British authorities concluded no ship could have survived the iceberg impact. They determined that the *Titanic* had been speeding through the icy waters too fast. Experts first believed the iceberg had ripped a 300-foot (90-m) gash in the side of the ship's hull. But it wasn't until deep-sea explorers finally discovered the wreck in 1985 that questions were raised about the ship's design. Part of the ship was buried, but sonar scans revealed that the holes from the iceberg were actually fairly small: six thin tears totaling about 12 square feet (1 sq m)—less than the size of two sidewalk squares. If it weren't for design mistakes that resulted in the *Titanic* taking on water faster, the doomed ship might have survived long enough for help to arrive.

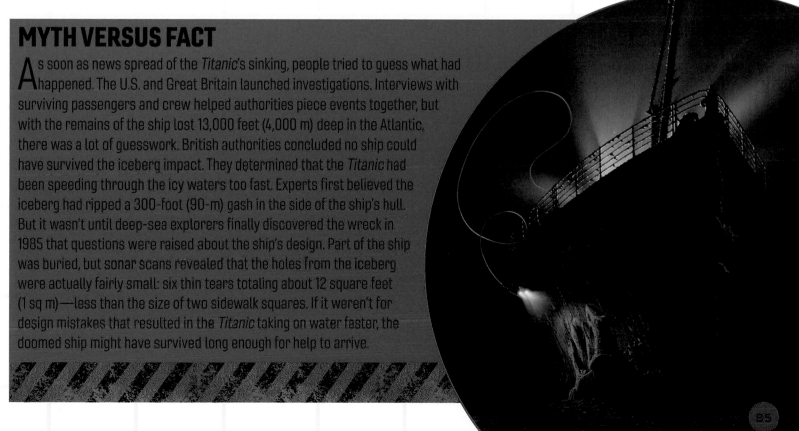

STICKY SITUATION

What caused a DEADLY FLOOD of oozing goo?

You're walking down the street and hear a rushing sound.

You look up to see a massive wave of sweet, sticky liquid hurtling toward you. You have just enough time to think "No way" before you're swept away in the liquid sugar. That's what happened in 1919, when a gigantic tank of molasses burst in Boston, Massachusetts. A tidal wave of sludge poured into the streets, smashing buildings and sweeping people off their feet. The event became known as the Great Boston Molasses Flood, and engineers remember it well: It taught them lessons that still matter more than a century after the sticky mess was cleaned up.

Why did the disaster happen?

Why was the molasses wave so destructive?

What did engineers learn from the disaster?

The Great Molasses Flood

It was an unusually warm Wednesday in January 1919. People in Boston's North End neighborhood were enjoying their afternoon. Workers were relaxing and eating lunch outside. They weren't paying much attention to the five-story steel storage tank sitting between buildings down the street. Suddenly, around 12:40 p.m., people heard a loud rumble. The giant tank burst open, and a wave of dark, sticky molasses gushed out. The wave was 15 to 40 feet (6 to 12 m) high and traveled up to 35 miles an hour (56 km/h). More than two million gallons (7.6 million L) of thick molasses flooded two city blocks. The goo knocked down elevated train tracks and swept buildings off their foundations, killing 21 people and injuring more than 150 others. The resulting mess took several months to clean up.

What in the World?

People who survived the incident couldn't believe what they had seen. Officials immediately started trying to figure out what had gone wrong. The company that owned the molasses tank claimed that someone must have bombed it. But an investigation soon revealed that the tank simply wasn't strong enough to hold an estimated 12,000 to 14,000 tons (11,000 to 12,700 t) of warm molasses. The result was a disaster like nothing the world had ever seen.

FATAL FLAWS

The molasses tank was made of seven rings of steel held together with metal rivets. But problems with this design contributed to the tank's dramatic explosion.

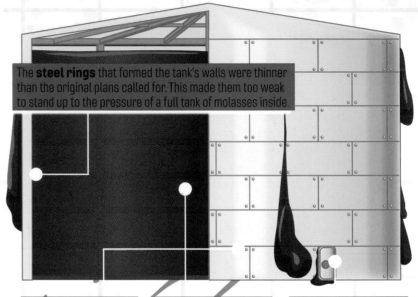

The **steel rings** that formed the tank's walls were thinner than the original plans called for. This made them too weak to stand up to the pressure of a full tank of molasses inside.

The builders used too few **rivets** to hold the steel rings together. As the heavy molasses pushed against the rivets, they started shooting out like missiles from the side of the tank.

As the molasses sat in the tank, it began fermenting—microbes like yeast ate the sugar and turned it into **gas.** This gas likely built up inside the tank and added to the pressure inside.

A **doorway** had been installed in the side of the bottom ring of the tank so workers could enter and clean it when it was empty. But this created a weak spot where the tank's steel walls began to crack.

>>> The molasses tank had been LEAKING from the seams for months. Instead of fixing it, the owners PAINTED THE TANK BROWN so the seeping syrup would be HARDER TO SEE.

TRY THIS!

Don't have a giant molasses tank handy? You can investigate the effects of fluid pressure with an empty milk carton at home. Have an adult poke two holes in the carton with a knife or sharp pencil. One hole should be about two inches (5 cm) from the bottom of the carton, and the other should be about two inches (5 cm) from the top. Hold a finger over each hole and fill the carton with water (an extra set of hands is helpful here). Then place the carton on the edge of the sink with the holes pointing into the basin. Remove your fingers and watch the water shoot out of the holes. The stream shooting farther is the one that has more fluid pressure above it.

MILK

TELL ME MORE

A PRESSING ISSUE

How could a stiff metal like steel be too weak to hold in gooey molasses? Why did it matter that the doorway was cut in the bottom, not the top? The answer to both of these questions has to do with fluid pressure—the force inside a body of liquid. If you've ever dived to the bottom of a swimming pool, you've felt fluid pressure from the water above pushing down on you. The deeper into a pool—or vat of molasses—you get, the more fluid there is above, pushing downward. With a heavy liquid like molasses, the strength of this downward push grows especially quickly. When the tank was only partly full, the pressure at the bottom was weak enough that the flawed tank could hold. But when the tank was filled—and gases started building up, pushing on the molasses even more—the downward pressure became too much for the tank to take.

One problem that doomed the molasses tank: The company that built it didn't consult an engineer, and the company miscalculated how much molasses the tank would be able to hold. After the disaster, new laws were made requiring licensed engineers to sign off on all major projects. Designers also had to show their calculations to authorities to double-check. These rules are still in place today, and they make everybody safer.

FUN FACTS

>>> The series of **TRIALS** to determine who was responsible for the **DISASTER** took nearly **SIX YEARS,** and more than 3,000 people testified. It was the **BIGGEST LEGAL BATTLE** in the city's history.

>>> The molasses that poured out of the ruptured tank was enough to fill more than **THREE** Olympic-size **SWIMMING POOLS.**

UNDER PRESSURE

The deeper a tank of fluid is, the more pressure there is at the bottom. When the fluid is ultra-thick molasses, the pressure packs a lot of punch.

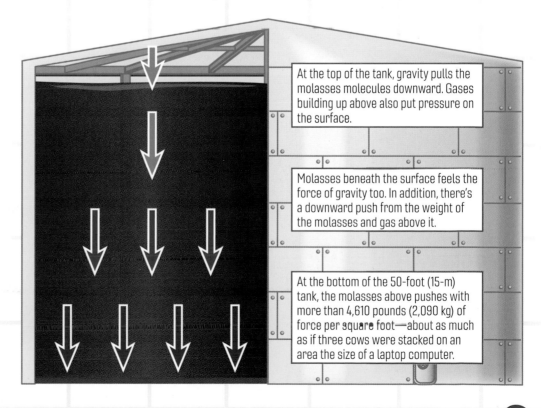

At the top of the tank, gravity pulls the molasses molecules downward. Gases building up above also put pressure on the surface.

Molasses beneath the surface feels the force of gravity too. In addition, there's a downward push from the weight of the molasses and gas above it.

At the bottom of the 50-foot (15-m) tank, the molasses above pushes with more than 4,610 pounds (2,090 kg) of force per square foot—about as much as if three cows were stacked on an area the size of a laptop computer.

We've Got a Job to Do

When a ship sinks, a building collapses, or a popular product injures people, everyone wants to know what happened. Was it an accident? Who was at fault? Could anyone have seen it coming—or prevented it? These questions are especially pressing if anyone was hurt. But if all that's left is a pile of rubble, answers can be hard to find.

> ## " WHEN THINGS WE DESIGN FAIL, IT'S IMPORTANT THAT WE CAN FIGURE OUT WHY, TO PREVENT THAT FROM HAPPENING AGAIN. "

That's where Jahan Rasty comes in. Rasty is a professor at Texas Tech University and a forensic engineer. He investigates structures and products that have fallen apart to figure out what went wrong. He's looked at faulty fences, burned-down buildings, and even hip implants that broke inside people's bodies. His goal: Figure out what happened so we can make things safer.

Rasty didn't set out to be a disaster detective. He originally studied how materials like metal react to being stressed and broken apart. "People would call the university and say, 'We have this thing that collapsed or this thing that exploded—could anybody help us figure out why?'" he says. "And those calls always got routed to me."

Rasty realized he could make a career out of investigating engineering problems. He started working with companies, government authorities, and lawyers who needed answers about how things broke down. Sometimes his investigations help prove people guilty or innocent in criminal trials. Other times, they help people who were injured by faulty products get compensated by companies that messed up.

To investigate an incident, Rasty starts by gathering evidence. He often collects pieces of the broken material to examine in his lab. Looking at fractured wood or metal under a microscope can help Rasty figure out if it was pushed, pulled, twisted, or blasted apart—and how quickly or slowly that happened. "All of those at the microscopic level leave different signatures," he says.

Looking at crime scenes and collapsed buildings isn't for everyone. But for Rasty, it's an essential part of making things better. "Humans are imperfect, and no system that we have is foolproof," he says. "When things we design fail, it's important that we can figure out why, to prevent that from happening again."

FORENSIC ENGINEERS NOT ONLY NEED TO BE GOOD AT **ENGINEERING.** THEY ALSO NEED TO WORK ON **PUBLIC SPEAKING,** SINCE THEY MAY TESTIFY IN **HUNDREDS** OF LEGAL TRIALS.

This concrete fencing became cracked and two panels completely fell apart. The reason? Steel support bars that weren't placed correctly.

Leaks from a damaged gas pipe like this one can cause fires and explosions.

On the Case

Forensic engineers can investigate everything from building collapses to broken household products. Here are a few things Jahan Rasty has analyzed.

Crumbling Concrete

Residents of a housing development called in Rasty when miles of concrete fencing around their homes fell apart after only two years. He determined that the concrete forms were built too weak, making the failed fences the manufacturer's fault.

Preventing Future Fires

In the mid-2010s, Rasty helped investigate what was behind a series of scary house fires. The forensic engineers found that gas pipes in the homes were too thin. That made it easier for them to spring leaks that lightning could then ignite.

Ladder Leader

Rasty often looks into collapsing ladders or tree stands—platforms that hunters attach to trees so they can sit high off the ground. Rasty's job is to determine whether these products failed because they were built poorly or because people used them incorrectly.

Hip Helper

Rasty has also analyzed failed hip implants—metal devices that doctors surgically implant in patients whose own hips no longer work right. If the implants break after only a few years, it could be because manufacturers didn't make them right.

UP IN FLAMES

How did a larger-than-life **AIRSHIP** meet its doom?

In 1937, it was the accident seen around the world: With news cameras rolling, an enormous flying airship called the *Hindenburg* suddenly burst into flames. Onlookers scrambled to get out of the way as the burning blimp crashed to the ground and its metal frame melted. One simple design change could have prevented the disaster, but the accident helped turn public opinion against airships for decades. What went wrong with the *Hindenburg*? Grab a pair of flight goggles, because we're heading skyward to find out.

How did airships work **?**

Why did the *Hindenburg* catch fire **?**

What would have prevented it **?**

I'm full of hot air!

JUST THE FACTS

Age of Airships

In the early 1900s, airplanes were just starting to take off. But travelers had another option: enormous balloon-like vehicles called airships. Airships used lighter-than-air lifting gas such as hydrogen or helium to carry passengers and cargo into the air. Particularly popular were rigid airships, called zeppelins, which had fabric stretched over a hard metal frame. The *Hindenburg,* launched in 1936, was the largest rigid airship ever constructed. At 804 feet (245 m) long and 135 feet (41 m) across, it could fit the entire Cathedral of Notre-Dame inside!

Crash and Burn

The *Hindenburg* was built in Germany and funded partly by the Nazi government in power at the time. By 1937, it had flown more than 200,000 miles (322,000 km) without any problems. On May 3, 1937, it was loaded with passengers traveling to the United States. Over the next three days, they sailed over the Atlantic, enjoying the spectacular views. But as the airship swooped in for a landing in Lakehurst, New Jersey, U.S.A., passengers heard a loud bang. The lifting gas that filled the zeppelin burst into flames, and the airship started falling. It crashed to the ground, and its metal frame crumpled as fire consumed the entire structure. From first spark to fiery collapse, the accident lasted just 34 seconds.

AIRSHIP ACCIDENT

The same gas that lifted the *Hindenburg* into the skies ultimately led to its destruction. Here's how it went down.

2. Inside the frame, 16 gas cells surrounded by protective mesh were pumped full of hydrogen to provide lift. Valves allowed the crew to release the gas gradually when they wanted to lower the ship.

1. Metal girders covered in fabric formed the frame of the airship.

3. As the ship came in for a landing, a spark caused a gas cell at the rear of the ship to catch fire. The fire quickly consumed all the hydrogen in the cell, and the back of the ship sank to the ground.

4. Flames ripped through the fabric exterior and quickly spread to the other 15 gas cells. As the front end fell, the fire spread, its heat destroying the zeppelin's metal frame.

>>> Despite the *Hindenburg*'s dramatic destruction, 62 OF THE 97 PEOPLE ON BOARD SURVIVED. When the front of the ship sank closer to the ground, they jumped out the windows, then ran away as fast as they could.

GOOD GAS, BAD GAS

Experts still disagree on exactly what started the *Hindenburg* fire. One theory is that hydrogen was leaking from the ship, and a spark from a lightning storm ignited the gas. But once the hydrogen started burning, there was no stopping it. And it definitely wouldn't have happened if the ship had been filled with helium instead. Both hydrogen and helium are lighter than air, but while hydrogen is highly flammable, helium is inert. In other words, it doesn't react to much of anything—including sparks. Helium is slightly less buoyant than hydrogen, so you'd need more of it, but it's much safer. Why didn't the Germans use it? They couldn't get their hands on any. The U.S., which produces most of the world's helium, wasn't exporting it at the time.

FUN FACTS

>>> The *Hindenburg* had a special **LIGHTWEIGHT PIANO** on board. It was made mostly of **ALUMINUM** rather than the usual heavy wood.

>>> Could **AIRSHIPS MAKE A COMEBACK?** Several companies have proposed building a new fleet of the **FLOATING VEHICLES** to move cargo around the world without burning **JET FUEL.**

>>> The *Hindenburg* had a cruising speed of **78 MILES AN HOUR** (126 km/h)—a little faster than a modern car **RACING** down the **FREEWAY.**

WHOA... SLOW DOWN.
A CLOSER LOOK AT COMBUSTION.

Combustion—the fancy word for something burning—is a chemical reaction. It typically requires three ingredients to get started: heat, oxygen, and fuel. When someone strikes a match, friction between the match head and the scratchy strike pad makes enough heat to create a spark. The spark helps molecules of fuel on the match head break apart and recombine with oxygen from the air, making light and heat. The reaction continues as long as there's more fuel to consume (like the wood in the match). Voilà! We have fire. But fuel doesn't have to be something solid. It can also be a gas, such as hydrogen, that combines easily with oxygen to make flames. Helium, on the other hand, doesn't easily combine with other elements. It's a much safer choice for your zeppelin.

LESSON LEARNED!
BUCKLING BRIDGE
NOVEMBER 7, 1940

The Incident

On a particularly windy day in Washington State, U.S.A., highway authorities had a problem. The suspension bridge across a channel called the Tacoma Narrows was wobbling wildly from side to side.

The bridge had opened just four months earlier. But people soon noticed that crossing it made them feel a little seasick. Even in a light breeze, the roadway wobbled, sometimes shaking enough to send visible ripples from one end to the other. This earned the Tacoma Narrows Bridge the nickname "Galloping Gertie."

Now, in winds upward of 42 miles an hour (68 km/h), the bridge began twisting like a ribbon. Its sides rose and fell up to 28 feet (9 m) every five seconds, throwing one of the last cars on the bridge against the curb. The swaying got worse and worse until onlookers could see the bottom of the bridge tipping upward. Bolts started breaking, cables started snapping, and chunks of concrete fell into the water below.

Finally, about an hour after the swaying started, a 600-foot (180-m) section of the bridge ripped off, flipped over, and crashed into the channel below. More pieces of the bridge deck followed, leaving a gaping hole where the middle of the bridge once was.

What Went Wrong

Engineers scrambled to figure out why the bridge had failed so catastrophically. In fact, experts are still arguing over the details, but some big problems quickly became clear. The bridge's lead builder, Leon Moisseiff, had decided to make the bridge lighter and narrower than originally planned to save some money on the epic project.

He also did away with the triangular metal trusses that usually run under the sides of a roadway and keep the bridge edges stiff. Instead, he used flat plates to strengthen the bridge's edges. But when the wind started blowing across the bridge, it pushed on these plates instead of passing through them, like it would have through triangular trusses.

The force of the wind started the lightweight bridge fluttering, like a blade of grass when you blow across its long edge. And as the bridge edge curved upward, it caught even more wind, making the effect worse. As the rippling grew, the bridge deck pulled and snapped some of the cables that were supposed to be steadying it, and the shaking turned into full-on twists and turns. The bridge was doomed.

THE BIG TAKEAWAY

THE TACOMA NARROWS BECAME ONE OF HISTORY'S MOST INFAMOUS STRUCTURAL FAILURES. Engineering students learn about it as an example of what not to do. That might be embarrassing for the bridge's designers—but it's an important example of how to learn from mistakes. Within months of the disaster, other engineers were already changing how they designed bridges. Now they make sure suspension bridges are streamlined from side to side so air can flow over them, and that they have stiff sections in the right places to resist twisting. Engineers also test smaller models of their designs in wind tunnels before building the real thing—just in case.

TIPPY TOWER

How did the **TOWER OF PISA** get its world-famous lean?

It's a tourist's delight—and an engineer's nightmare. The Leaning Tower of Pisa, whose construction started in the 1100s, looks more like an unsteady stack of blocks than the inspiring church tower it was meant to be. What caused this now popular attraction to tip sideways so dramatically? Did its builders know they were making such a colossal mistake? We're about to tackle the engineering of this structure—just try not to lose your balance.

Why is the tower leaning **?**

Didn't anyone try to fix it **?**

Is it going to fall **?**

JUST THE FACTS

Cursed Construction

Builders started the Tower of Pisa in the year 1173. By the time three out of eight planned stories were completed, it was already starting to lean. Then a war broke out in Italy, and construction paused—for about 100 years. When engineers finally finished the tower, they added extra bricks on one side to try to make the building appear straight. But this extra weight only made the situation worse. In 1370, when the tower was finally completed, it was unmistakably angled. Not exactly the magnificent structure its original architects had imagined.

That Sinking Feeling

More than 600 years later, the tower is still standing—but it looks like it might fall at any moment. It's leaning so badly that the top of the tower is more than 13 feet (4 m) farther south than the bottom. The main problem? The ground beneath Pisa is made mostly of mud, clay, and wet sand—none of which is stable. The simple stone foundation the builders used wasn't enough to support the nearly 16,000 tons (14,500 t) of marble the tower is made of. As a result, the massive structure is gradually sinking into the soggy ground below.

TOWER TIMELINE

Multiple attempts were made to right the Leaning Tower during its 200-year path to completion.

1173: Construction on the Tower of Pisa begins. It's designed to be a tall, straight tower with bells at the top.

1178: Having reached the third story, workers notice a slight lean in the building. Construction is paused to figure out a solution, but then Pisa goes to war.

1275: Work restarts with a new engineer in charge. When he takes over, the tower is leaning 0.2 degree to the north. He tries to compensate by building the new stories slightly taller on the short side.

1284: A new war interrupts construction again. At this point, seven of eight stories are complete—but after growing heavier and sinking deeper into its foundation, the tower is now tipping about one degree to the south.

1350: The lean has increased to 1.6 degrees south, and yet another architect begins work on the top of the tower. He tries to adjust for the lean by making the stairway longer on one side.

1370: The tower is officially completed, and the lean is dramatic—but the tower doesn't fall!

1817: After about 450 years of sinking, the tower leans nearly five degrees south.

1934: Italian dictator Benito Mussolini orders engineers to straighten the tower, which he sees as an embarrassment. They drill holes in the foundation and pour in concrete, but the tipping only gets worse.

1990: With a lean of 5.5 degrees, engineers calculate that the tower could fall at any moment. It's closed to the public for the next 11 years as workers straighten the foundation and finally stabilize the tower.

OFF KILTER

Multiple factors contributed to the precarious lean the Tower of Pisa has today.

Most of the tower is made of heavy white marble. With the extra bricks that architects added to try to fix the lean, it weighs almost 32 million pounds (14.5 million kg).

Pisa is near the coast of Italy. The loose sand and clay that make up the ground are constantly waterlogged and shift easily.

Builders dug only about six feet (2 m) deep to place the tower's underground foundation. The millions of pounds of marble above press these points deeper and deeper into the unstable muck.

FUN FACT >>> To save money, builders used CHEAPER LIMESTONE for the tower's BURIED SECTIONS. This may have actually helped it STAY UP, since limestone can FLEX slightly, bending instead of breaking as the lean pulls the tower to the side.

TELL ME MORE

LEAN INTO IT

Why hasn't the tower fallen over yet? It comes down to center of gravity. An object's center of gravity is the point where the weight around it is equal in every direction. As long as this point is still over the tower's base, the structure will stay up. In 1990, a team of engineers calculated that the tower would likely topple if its lean reached an angle of 5.44 degrees, bringing its center of gravity over the ground. At that point, it had actually tipped about 5.5 degrees—so they weren't sure how it was still standing, but they knew they had to act fast! For the next 11 years, the tower was closed as engineers scrambled to stabilize it. By removing some of the soil beneath the opposite side of the tower, they brought the lean back under four degrees, keeping the structure safe—at least for the next 200 years or so.

STAYING CENTERED

Because the Leaning Tower is thicker at the bottom than at the top, its center of gravity is located just below halfway up.

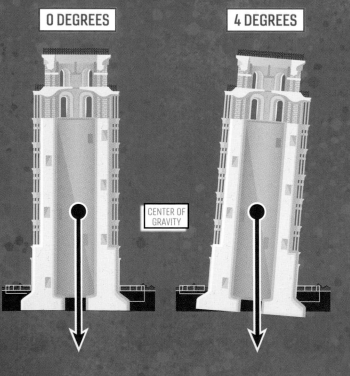

0 DEGREES	4 DEGREES

CENTER OF GRAVITY

AT A LEAN OF 4 DEGREES, the center of gravity is still directly above the tower's foundation. It doesn't look pretty, but the base supports the weight.

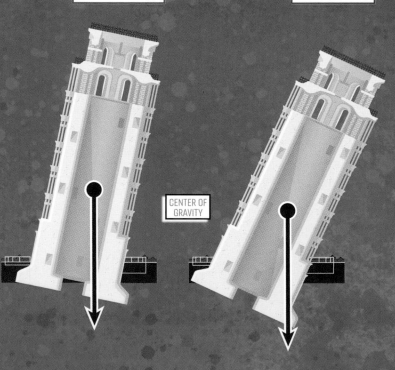

11.5 DEGREES	25 DEGREES

CENTER OF GRAVITY

IF THE LEAN GOES PAST 5.44 DEGREES, most of the tower's weight hangs over open air. The tower risks toppling as gravity pulls it toward the ground.

FUN FACTS

>>> The biggest of the tower's **SEVEN BELLS** weighs about **8,000 POUNDS** (3,600 kg). In the early 1900s, it was silenced, as workers worried its weight **ROCKING BACK AND FORTH** could worsen the tower's lean.

>>> In the **1990s,** nearly **TWO MILLION POUNDS** (900 t) of **LEAD COUNTERWEIGHTS** were added to the north side of the tower to help keep it from **TIPPING FURTHER.**

>>> Surprisingly, the **LEANING TOWER** has survived at least **FOUR STRONG EARTHQUAKES** since 1280. Engineers say the **WOBBLY FOUNDATION** helped absorb some of the vibrations, **KEEPING THE TOWER ITSELF SAFE.**

TRY THIS!

Make your own leaning towers. Set a stack of about three sheets of paper on a flat surface. Next, set an empty paper towel roll and an empty toilet paper roll standing upright at the edge of the paper, so that half of each roll is on the paper stack and half is off of it. Steadying the rolls with a hand if needed, carefully slide additional sheets of paper onto the pile beneath the rolls until the angle is too great and they fall over. How many sheets of paper were you able to add to the stack before the tilting rolls finally fell? Which roll fell first?

MYTH VERSUS FACT

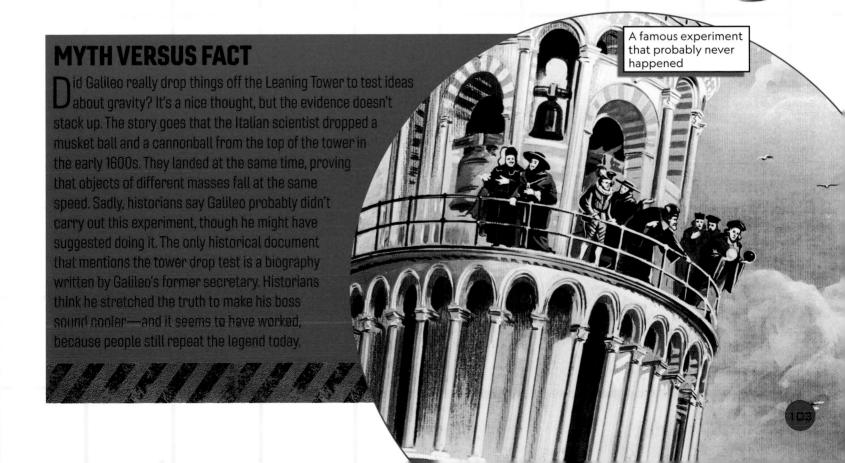

A famous experiment that probably never happened

Did Galileo really drop things off the Leaning Tower to test ideas about gravity? It's a nice thought, but the evidence doesn't stack up. The story goes that the Italian scientist dropped a musket ball and a cannonball from the top of the tower in the early 1600s. They landed at the same time, proving that objects of different masses fall at the same speed. Sadly, historians say Galileo probably didn't carry out this experiment, though he might have suggested doing it. The only historical document that mentions the tower drop test is a biography written by Galileo's former secretary. Historians think he stretched the truth to make his boss sound cooler—and it seems to have worked, because people still repeat the legend today.

SINKING STADIUM

Why did a Minnesota SPORTS ARENA collapse in on itself?

In the U.S., in early December 2010, Minnesota Vikings fans were looking forward to a big football game between their home team and the New York Giants. But then something got in the way: the roof of their stadium. It collapsed completely in a blizzard. The game had to be moved to Michigan, two whole states away. Why couldn't the soaring stadium withstand a little snowfall? The answer is all about air, so take a deep breath and let's jump in.

How did the Metrodome's roof work ?

How did workers try to save it ?

Why did it collapse ?

JUST THE FACTS

Keeping It Light

Many sports stadiums have domed roofs held up by stiff metal supports called trusses. But in the late 1970s, when construction started on the Metrodome, inflatable roofs were all the rage instead. The Metrodome's top was made of 10 acres (4 ha) of thin, flexible fabric coated in ultra-tough Teflon. It was held up entirely by air that was constantly pumped into the stadium, keeping the roof inflated like a balloon. The stadium's engineers knew that building a domed roof with trusses would be stronger. But inflatable roofs were faster to install and required less material. Sounds good, right?

Sunk by Snow

The Metrodome roof was usually heated to keep snow from collecting on top. Any snow that built up slid down the curved sides of the dome. While this was usually enough to make it through a Minnesota winter, the blizzard in 2010 dumped about 17 inches (43 cm) of heavy wet snow on the stadium over a short time period. Workers tried to melt it by spraying the roof with hot water, but it was too late. The weight of the snow tore the thin fabric, and the roof rapidly deflated. Snow dumped into the inside of the stadium as the roof fluttered to the ground.

FUN FACT >>> Is it possible that the METRODOME'S BUILDERS didn't expect it to SNOW much? Not really—the city of Minneapolis receives an average of 4.6 FEET (1.4 m) of snow every year!

BIG BUBBLE

The key to holding the Metrodome's roof up was keeping more air moving into the stadium than out of it.

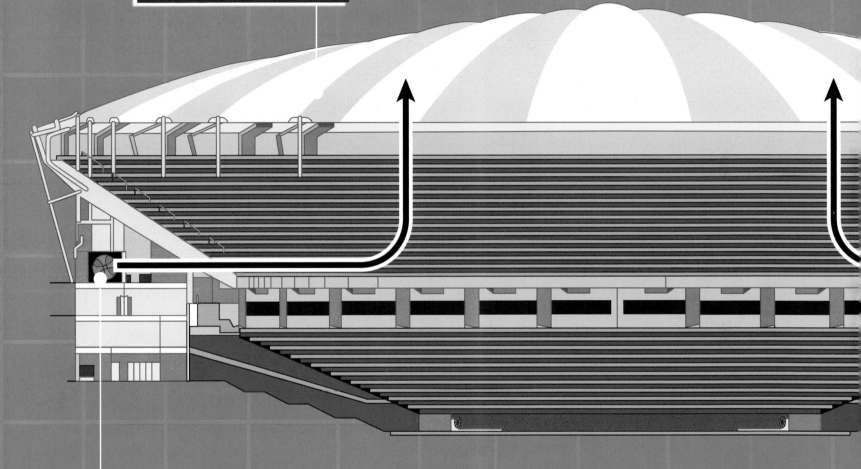

A **fabric roof** just .05 inch (1.3 mm) thick stretched across the top of the stadium. A coating of Teflon strengthened the fabric and made it slippery, so rain and snow would slide off.

Twenty massive **fans** (the propeller kind, not the cheering kind) blew air from outside the stadium into it, keeping the roof dome inflated. They pumped in enough air to fill an Olympic-size swimming pool every minute.

Revolving doors helped keep air inside the stadium as spectators entered and exited. But some air still escaped, so the fans had to stay on at all times.

FUN FACT >> An INFLATABLE ROOF may have saved some MONEY during construction. But by 2010, stadium owners were paying $60,000 A MONTH just to run the fans that kept the roof up!

TELL ME MORE

PRESSURE'S ON

The Metrodome used the principles of air pressure to stay inflated. To keep the roof up, the pressure on the roof from the inside needed to be greater than the pressure outside. Air molecules are like people in an elevator: They don't bunch together unless they have to, but instead spread out until the space between them is even. As the air inside the stadium tried to expand, it pushed on the flexible fabric of the roof dome. But as soon as the roof was punctured, it was like opening the elevator doors—the air that was pushing against the dome rushed out.

TRY THIS!

Just how strong is air pressure? Fill a glass about a third full with water. Place a square of cardstock or an index card over the mouth of the glass so that it completely covers the opening. Over a sink, hold your hand over the card and turn the glass over so that the mouth is now facing down. Take your hand off the index card. The air pressure pushing up on the card should be stronger than the pressure of the water in the glass pushing down on it, keeping the water inside the glass.

FUN FACTS

>>> Earth's **ATMOSPHERE** is constantly putting **PRESSURE** on us. At sea level, it's pushing on every square inch with **14.7 POUNDS** (6.7 kg) of force—but because it's even all over, we don't usually notice it.

>>> The **METRODOME** wasn't the only stadium of its kind to fizzle. The University of Northern Iowa, U.S.A., replaced the **INFLATABLE ROOF** of its football stadium with a rigid one after it **COLLAPSED.**

>>> A former Metrodome worker once admitted to secretly **ADJUSTING THE VENTILATION SYSTEM** during baseball games. He wanted the blowing air to make balls fly farther when the home team was at bat. **(DEFINITELY CHEATING!)**

AIR ESCAPE! The Metrodome's roof deflated as air molecules from inside the stadium raced to find space to spread out.

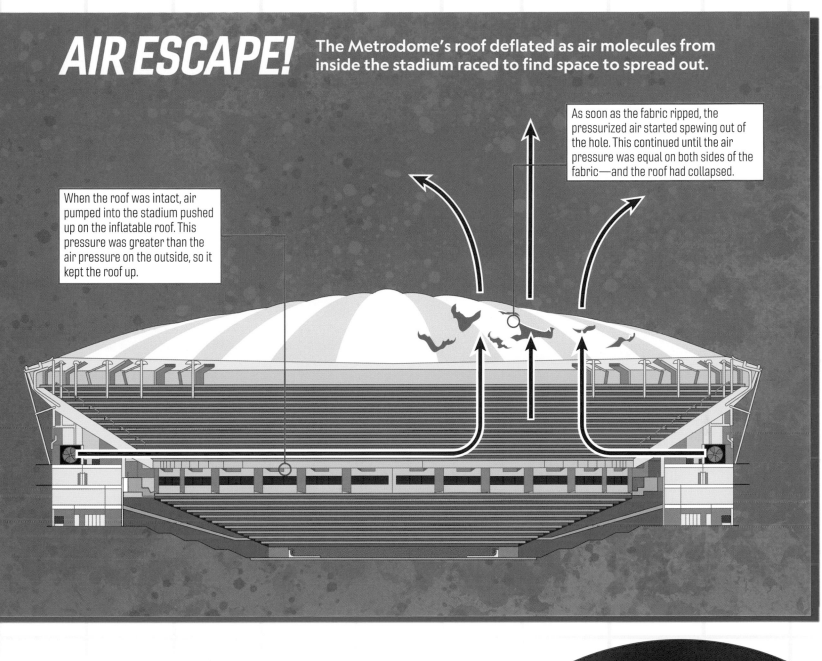

As soon as the fabric ripped, the pressurized air started spewing out of the hole. This continued until the air pressure was equal on both sides of the fabric—and the roof had collapsed.

When the roof was intact, air pumped into the stadium pushed up on the inflatable roof. This pressure was greater than the air pressure on the outside, so it kept the roof up.

WHOA... SLOW DOWN.
A CLOSER LOOK AT AIR PRESSURE.

Air pressure can be hard to picture—especially because air itself is invisible. But you've felt it anytime you've tried to walk into a heavy wind. That force you feel pushing back against you? That's the power of all the air molecules beating against your skin. The more molecules there are—and the closer they're packed together—the more force they create as they race around trying to spread out. By pumping air into the Metrodome and forcing the trapped molecules to crowd together more closely than they did outside the stadium, engineers increased the pressure. This created the push that kept the stadium roof up.

NOT-SO-GREAT PYRAMIDS

How did COLLAPSING PYRAMIDS pave the way for the marvels that stand now?

Most people know the Great Pyramid of Giza and the other perfectly pointy structures commissioned by ancient Egyptian pharaohs. But how did anyone know how to build such colossal structures back then? Well, it took a few bent, broken, and busted pyramids to get there. Keep an eye out for falling rock, because we're about to take a closer look.

What did early pyramids look like?

What went wrong with their construction?

How did pyramid designers learn from them?

JUST THE FACTS

High Hopes

Many Egyptian pharaohs wanted to be buried beneath impressive pyramids when they died. The earliest were step pyramids, with rectangular layers that rested on top of each other and got smaller as they went up. That's how builders originally planned to make the Meidum Pyramid. But around 2575 B.C., when they'd already started building it, a new pharaoh named Snefru decided he wanted it to have smooth sides instead. This didn't exactly work out.

Falling Face

Building a smooth-faced pyramid out of precisely cut stone blocks is tricky. The blocks have to press against each other at just the right angle to keep the entire structure from collapsing under its own weight. Unfortunately, ancient engineers didn't understand this when they tried to tack a smooth face onto the outer layers of the Meidum Pyramid. The additional stone eventually fell off and formed a pile of rubble at the pyramid's base. No one knows exactly when this happened, or whether Snefru was still alive to see it. But the failure of the design is pretty obvious today.

PYRAMIDS WORLDWIDE

Ancient peoples around the world discovered that pyramids were a good way to build tall structures—and over centuries, they learned to build them right.

CIRCA 2620 B.C. The first step pyramid is built in ancient Egypt. It consists of six layers of stone that get successively smaller, reaching a total of 200 feet (61 m) high.

CIRCA 2551 B.C. The Great Pyramid, built for Snefru's son Pharaoh Khufu, takes more than two million stones to build. At 481 feet (147 m) high, it remains the tallest structure on Earth for more than 3,000 years.

CIRCA A.D. 100 Ancient people in Mexico build a 216-foot (66-m) pyramid in Teotihuacán, Mexico. Now called the Pyramid of the Sun, it's one of the largest structures of its kind in the Western Hemisphere.

CIRCA A.D. 350 People in modern-day Sudan finish building about 40 tall, skinny pyramids in which to bury royalty. Scholars think the pyramids may have had stone spheres on top, but that these have fallen off.

CIRCA A.D. 600 The Maya people of what's now Guatemala build the Pyramids of Tikal to hold their religious rituals. The tallest rises 213 feet (65 m) and has a temple on top.

FUN FACT Why be BURIED in a pyramid? Egyptian pharaohs believed they'd BECOME GODS after death. Pyramids showed their power—and gave them ROOM TO STORE ALL THE THINGS they'd need to rule in the NEXT WORLD.

LAYERING UP

Snefru wanted to keep adding to the Meidum Pyramid—an ambitious plan that ultimately proved to be a mistake.

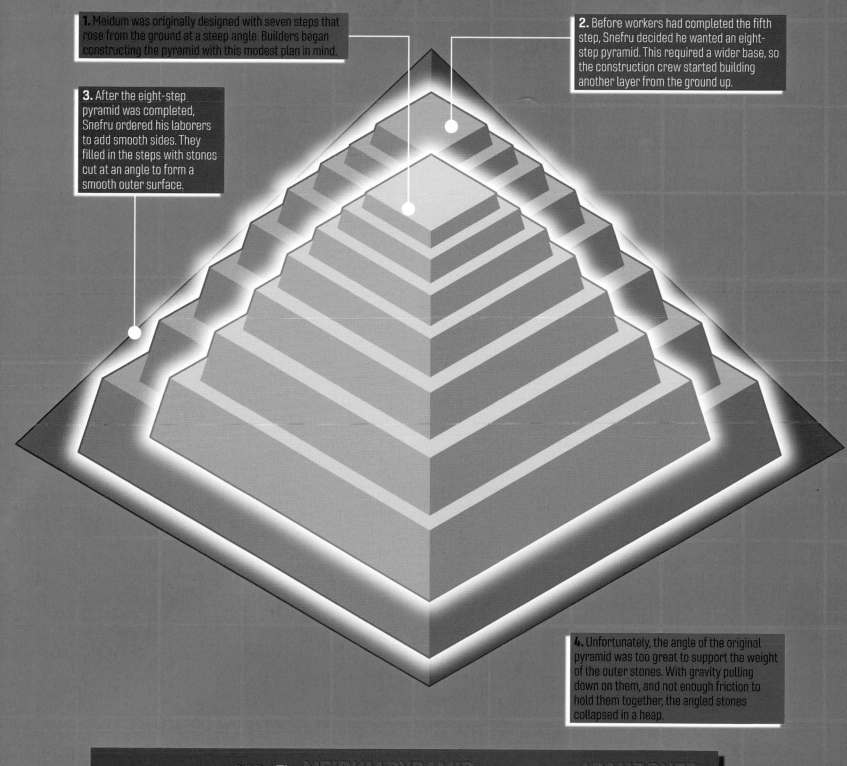

1. Meidum was originally designed with seven steps that rose from the ground at a steep angle. Builders began constructing the pyramid with this modest plan in mind.

2. Before workers had completed the fifth step, Snefru decided he wanted an eight-step pyramid. This required a wider base, so the construction crew started building another layer from the ground up.

3. After the eight-step pyramid was completed, Snefru ordered his laborers to add smooth sides. They filled in the steps with stones cut at an angle to form a smooth outer surface.

4. Unfortunately, the angle of the original pyramid was too great to support the weight of the outer stones. With gravity pulling down on them, and not enough friction to hold them together, the angled stones collapsed in a heap.

FUN FACT >>> The MEIDUM PYRAMID may have been ABANDONED before it was even finished. It's hard for archaeologists and historians to piece together what happened because OVER THE CENTURIES, ROBBERS carried many of the fallen stones away.

TELL ME MORE

TRY, TRY AGAIN

Pharaoh Snefru didn't give up on pyramids after the failure at Meidum. He commissioned another at a nearby site called Dahshur. This one was designed to be a true flat-faced pyramid. But midway through construction, cracks started appearing in its structure. Builders realized that the angle at which the pyramid was rising was too steep. They switched to a less steep angle to keep the pyramid from collapsing, which left it with what looks like a shrunken top. It's now known as the Bent Pyramid.

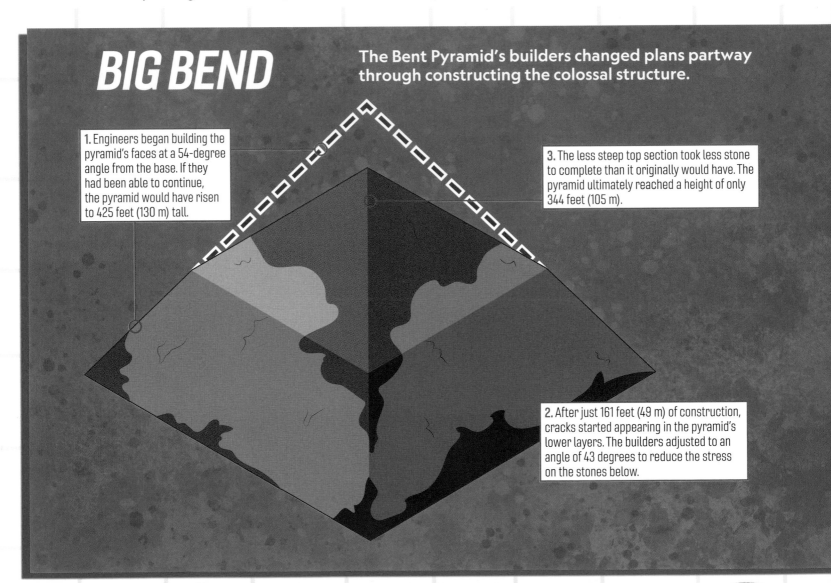

BIG BEND

The Bent Pyramid's builders changed plans partway through constructing the colossal structure.

1. Engineers began building the pyramid's faces at a 54-degree angle from the base. If they had been able to continue, the pyramid would have risen to 425 feet (130 m) tall.

3. The less steep top section took less stone to complete than it originally would have. The pyramid ultimately reached a height of only 344 feet (105 m).

2. After just 161 feet (49 m) of construction, cracks started appearing in the pyramid's lower layers. The builders adjusted to an angle of 43 degrees to reduce the stress on the stones below.

TRY THIS!

Just how steep can a pyramid get before the force of gravity becomes greater than the forces holding the pile together? Make sloped piles with a few different grainy materials (like salt, sugar, and sand) to find out. Can a pile of sugar get steeper than a pile of salt? What about a pile of sand? Do the piles of thicker grains have steeper or shallower angles?

FUN FACTS

>>> **SNEFRU'S ENGINEERS** seem to have learned from their **MISTAKES.** After the **BENT PYRAMID,** they built him the first successful flat-faced pyramid—the Red Pyramid—which **INSPIRED THE GREAT PYRAMID** and others we know today.

>>> After remaining **OFF-LIMITS** for decades, the Bent Pyramid opened to tourists in 2019. Visitors can **EXPLORE** two of the pyramid's inner chambers—just watch out for the **GHOSTS** of frustrated engineers. (Kidding!)

>>> Two of Snefru's sons were buried near the **MEIDUM PYRAMID.** But to this day, archaeologists haven't found the **PHARAOH'S** own remains.

A passage inside the Bent Pyramid

Bent Pyramid of King Snefru

The Meidum Pyramid

A man walks through a passage inside the Bent Pyramid.

MYTH VERSUS FACT

How did laborers lift heavy stones to build the pyramids? Each block weighed tons—too massive to move without assistance. Some people think aliens swung by to help. (Seems unlikely.) But in 2018, a team of archaeologists found the remains of an ancient ramp with staircases on either side. The ramp had holes where workers could have mounted sturdy posts. Experts think the builders moved these ramps up to the face of the pyramid, changing the slope as the pyramid grew. Then they rigged ropes around the posts to make a pulley system, which would reduce the force it took to haul the heavy stones to the top.

An up-close look at the huge blocks that make up the pyramids in Egypt

TRY THIS!

INCREDIBLE EDIBLE EDIFICE

USE PASTA AND MARSHMALLOWS TO BUILD A STRONG TOWER—THEN WATCH IT FALL

You're an engineer who's competing for a special project. To get it, you have to prove your skills. Using only a handful of ingredients, build a platform as tall as you can that can hold as much weight as possible. You'll need to use your wits and knowledge, and items not usually known for their strength. Ready ... set ... build!

WHAT YOU NEED

TIME: 30 minutes

1. One package dried spaghetti (about 16 ounces or 450 g)

2. One package regular-size marshmallows (not mini)

3. Several paperback or thin hardcover books

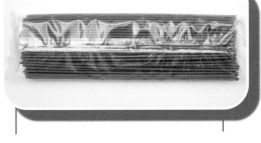

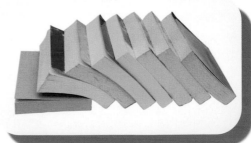

116

1. Set out the spaghetti and marshmallows—these are your building supplies.

2. Try poking a piece of spaghetti into one of the marshmallows. You may have to experiment with how hard to push to get the pasta to stick in the marshmallow without breaking.

3. Start building! A few ideas to try: Use a few pieces of spaghetti together in some spots. Snap the pasta into smaller pieces to make it easier to work with. Use triangles of spaghetti and marshmallows to add strength to your design.

4. When your structure is as high as you think it can get while still remaining strong, begin piling on the paperback books (gently!). How many can you add before the structure snaps or topples?

1

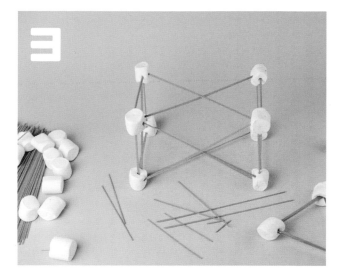

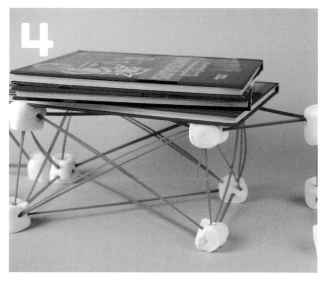

4

WHAT TO EXPECT

EVENTUALLY, WITH ENOUGH WEIGHT PUSHING DOWN ON IT, YOUR STRUCTURE WILL BREAK. THERE'S ONLY SO MUCH FORCE THAT BRITTLE SPAGHETTI AND THOSE SQUISHY MARSHMALLOWS CAN WITHSTAND. BUT WHEN THE BIG CRASH HAPPENS, YOU GET TO PUT ON YOUR FORENSIC ENGINEER HAT. TAKE A CLOSE LOOK AT YOUR COLLAPSED MASTERPIECE. CAN YOU SEE WHERE IT STARTED TO BREAK FIRST? WHERE WERE THE WEAK SPOTS? WHAT CAN YOU DO TO MAKE THEM STRONGER NEXT TIME?

WHAT'S GOING ON?

BUILDING STRUCTURES IS ALL ABOUT BALANCING FORCES. THE FORCE OF GRAVITY IS PULLING DOWN ON THE BOOKS, PUTTING PRESSURE ON YOUR BUILDING MATERIALS. YOU NEED A DESIGN THAT CAN WITHSTAND THIS PRESSURE. THAT'S WHY BUILDING WITH TRIANGLES WORKS SO WELL—WHEN FORCE IS APPLIED TO THE TOP POINT OF A TRIANGLE, IT SPREADS EVENLY THROUGH ALL THREE SIDES, MAKING IT HARDER TO BREAK. DID YOU NOTICE THAT A FEW PIECES OF SPAGHETTI BUNDLED TOGETHER ARE STRONGER THAN A SINGLE PIECE? THAT'S BECAUSE THE FORCES OF COMPRESSION AND TENSION ARE NO LONGER PUSHING ON JUST ONE PIECE. TOGETHER, THEY MAKE A THICKER PIECE THAT'S HARDER TO SNAP.

CHAPTER 4

DESTRUCTIVE BY NATURE

Sure, people are pretty good at making things fall apart.

BUT YOU KNOW WHAT WAS DOING IT BILLIONS OF YEARS BEFORE WE SHOWED UP?

Planet Earth itself. From crumbling mountainsides to insanely ravenous animals, nature has thousands of ways to wreak destruction. But this also comes with opportunities to build things back up—and, for us puny people, a chance to learn how it all works. Strap yourself in, because we're about to see what our mighty planet is capable of doing.

SWALLOWED UP

Why do GIANT HOLES suddenly open up in the earth?

It sounds like something from a sci-fi movie: A gaping hole suddenly opens in the ground, swallowing vehicles, buildings, and anything else nearby. But this bizarro phenomenon actually happens on our home planet. We're talking about sinkholes— those deep chasms that can appear in cities and the countryside, sometimes with little warning. Let's take a closer look at how these freaky landforms operate. Watch your step!

What are sinkholes **?**

How do they form **?**

How dangerous are they **?**

JUST THE FACTS

Sinkhole Surprise

One fall morning in 2018 in New Zealand, a farmworker woke up before dawn. He set out on his motorbike to round up cows for milking. But he found something unexpected out in the pasture: a chasm 656 feet (200 m) long and as deep as a six-story building that hadn't been there the day before. He almost drove right in! The sudden rift was a sinkhole—and geologists think it had been forming invisibly for decades before opening up overnight.

Washed Away

How did this otherworldly event take shape? It has to do with the bedrock—the layer of Earth beneath the soil. In some parts of the world, the bedrock is made of material that dissolves easily in water. As rain seeps into it, parts of the bedrock erode—they wear away. The soil above starts sinking into the cavity that is created. Usually this happens gradually, leaving bowl-like depressions in the ground or pools that fill with water. But sometimes underground cavities remain covered by a thin layer of rock and soil as they grow enormous—until the ground above them finally collapses, forming a sudden and spectacular "cover-collapse" sinkhole.

SINKHOLE HALL OF FAME

Most sinkholes form gradually. But when the collapses come out of nowhere, the news quickly travels around the world.

In 2010, leaky pipes and tropical storm rains washed away the loose rock under a neighborhood in Guatemala City, Guatemala. The ground collapsed into a hole 30 stories deep, swallowing a small factory and several telephone poles.

In 2014, employees of the National Corvette Museum in Bowling Green, Kentucky, U.S.A., were surprised to find that a sinkhole had formed in the middle of the museum—and eight of the expensive sports cars had been sucked in!

A Pittsburgh, Pennsylvania, U.S.A., bus driver and his only passenger were startled in 2019 when they were stopped at a light and the back of the bus suddenly lurched downward. The street under the back of the bus had collapsed, and the bus's rear end had fallen in.

Following a 6.4-magnitude quake on December 29, 2020, dozens of sinkholes began to open around Mecencani, Croatia. Frequent aftershock quakes continued to rattle the area for months, causing more than 100 sinkholes to appear.

OPEN UP!

Cover-collapse sinkholes are the rarest but most dangerous type. Here's how they form.

1. As rain falls through the air, it absorbs carbon dioxide, which makes it slightly acidic.

2. Acidic water trickles through the soil and dissolves the bedrock beneath it, forming a cavity.

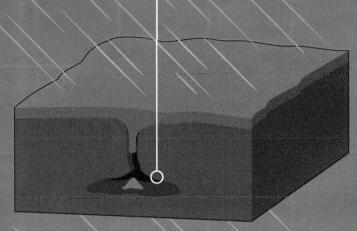

3. Some soil falls into the cavity, but some of it sticks together to form a bridge over the hole.

4. As more soil falls, the bridge gets thinner, but the cavity remains invisible from aboveground.

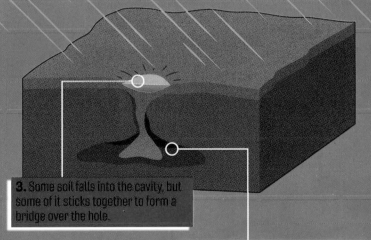

5. When the bridge gets thin enough, or weighed down by heavy rain, it collapses into the cavity to form a sudden and dramatic sinkhole.

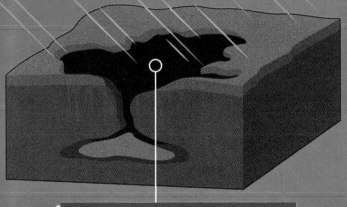

FUN FACT

>>> The world's DEEPEST KNOWN SINKHOLE is in southern China. The 128,000-YEAR-OLD Xiaozhai Tiankeng, or Heavenly Pit, plunges 2,172 FEET (662 m)—deep enough to fit the Empire State Building with PLENTY of room to spare.

TELL ME MORE

LEAKY LANDSCAPES

Feeling suspicious of the ground beneath you? Fair enough. But sinkholes can't appear just anywhere—they need a specific kind of bedrock under the soil. Hard rock, like granite, won't form sinkholes. But softer rocks like limestone and gypsum dissolve in slightly acidic water, leaving behind caverns and crevices that set the stage for natural sinkholes to form. Scientists call this kind of landscape karst. There are benefits: Some of the underground openings in the karst collect water, which people can tap into for drinking or irrigation. But sinkholes and other dramatic land changes also occur much more often in these conditions than in harder rock.

FULL OF HOLES

Water flowing through karst carves out all sorts of fantastical formations beyond sinkholes, including twisting caves and disappearing streams.

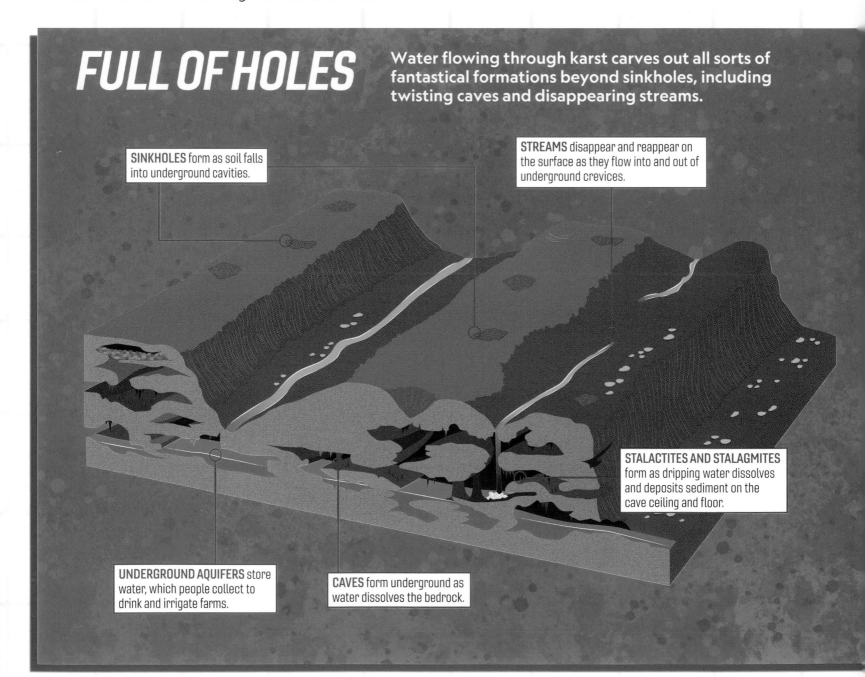

SINKHOLES form as soil falls into underground cavities.

STREAMS disappear and reappear on the surface as they flow into and out of underground crevices.

STALACTITES AND STALAGMITES form as dripping water dissolves and deposits sediment on the cave ceiling and floor.

UNDERGROUND AQUIFERS store water, which people collect to drink and irrigate farms.

CAVES form underground as water dissolves the bedrock.

FUN FACTS

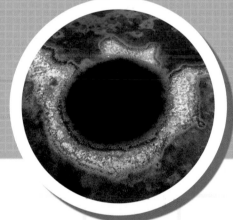

>>> Air **POLLUTION** can make rainwater more **ACIDIC**—which scientists say probably **SPEEDS UP** the rate at which **HOLES** form.

>>> In some places, the water underground **ACTUALLY *PREVENTS* SINKHOLES.** When **TOO MUCH WATER** is pumped out of underground aquifers for cities to use or for **IRRIGATING CROPS,** then the ground can collapse.

Sharp spikes of limestone in Madagascar

>>> On the **AFRICAN ISLAND OF MADAGASCAR,** water has eroded limestone, leaving behind a towering **"FOREST"** of jagged **LIMESTONE SHARDS.**

>>> The **GREAT BLUE HOLE** in Belize is the **LARGEST UNDERWATER SINKHOLE** in the world. Over thousands of years, a series of **CAVERNS COLLAPSED,** creating a pool that's **400 FEET (121 M) DEEP** in the middle of a shallow reef.

MYTH VERSUS FACT

Are you really at risk of suddenly being swallowed? Thankfully, the odds are incredibly slim. Here's why: Sinkholes are rare to begin with. If one does appear, odds are that it will be in a rural area without many people around to fall in. Plus, most sinkholes form gradually, and they come with plenty of warning signs. Sagging land, cracking roads or walls, and leaning trees or telephone poles can all be signals that an underground chasm is growing—and can give people time to get out of the way. So, sure, be on the lookout if you know you live in a sinkhole-prone area. But otherwise it's probably not worth thinking too deeply about.

SHAKE IT UP

Where do **EARTHQUAKES** get their destructive power?

The ground beneath our feet isn't always solid. One way it likes to demonstrate that: by moving everything above it in a rock-breaking, building-wobbling, nerve-rattling earthquake. These shaky situations can be pretty alarming—but there's also a lot we can learn from them. Get ready to rumble.

Why do earthquakes happen?

What causes the shaking?

How can we make buildings and cities safer?

LOL
whoops.

JUST THE FACTS

Feeling Shaky

About every minute, there's an earthquake somewhere on the planet. Most are minor tremors too small, or too deep in the ocean, for people to feel. But every year there are also hundreds of bigger quakes—some that just rattle the dishes and others that uproot trees, buckle roads, and tip buildings on their sides if they aren't earthquake proof. Though scientists have a good sense of where these big shakes are likely to happen, predicting when they'll hit is much harder.

On the Move

Earthquakes happen because Earth's upper layers are always moving. What we think of as solid ground and seafloor is actually divided into 12 main slabs of land known as tectonic plates. These plates drift slowly on top of the hot, flowing mantle. When they collide, they grind against each other, building up huge amounts of stress and pressure that are eventually released as earthquakes. Think of them like big, slow barges that are constantly crashing into each other. You can imagine that things would get a little shaky on deck.

BUILDING BY SHAKING

Earthquakes are best known for knocking things down. But tectonic plates also create new—and extremely cool—landforms as they rattle the ground.

The world's tallest mountains, the Himalaya, rose more than 23,000 feet (7,000 m) as India's tectonic plate pushed into Asia's over 50 million years. Frequent earthquakes are a sign that the mountains continue to grow.

Quakes often rattle the Afar region in Ethiopia as the churning mantle wells up and pushes two tectonic plates away from each other. In 2005, a series of cracks opened up between them. Within a million years, water will flow in from the Red Sea, and a new ocean will form.

Ocean trenches form as one tectonic plate plunges underneath another. The deepest, darkest parts of these underwater trenches are the sites of some of the largest known earthquakes.

The Mariana Trench is the deepest ocean trench in the world.

FUN FACT

The effects of a 1964 MEGA-QUAKE in Alaska, which measured 9.2 IN MAGNITUDE, helped geologists prove that their emerging theory of PLATE TECTONICS was true.

GRINDING GROUND

At a transform boundary, two tectonic plates scrape together sideways, resulting in many earthquakes.

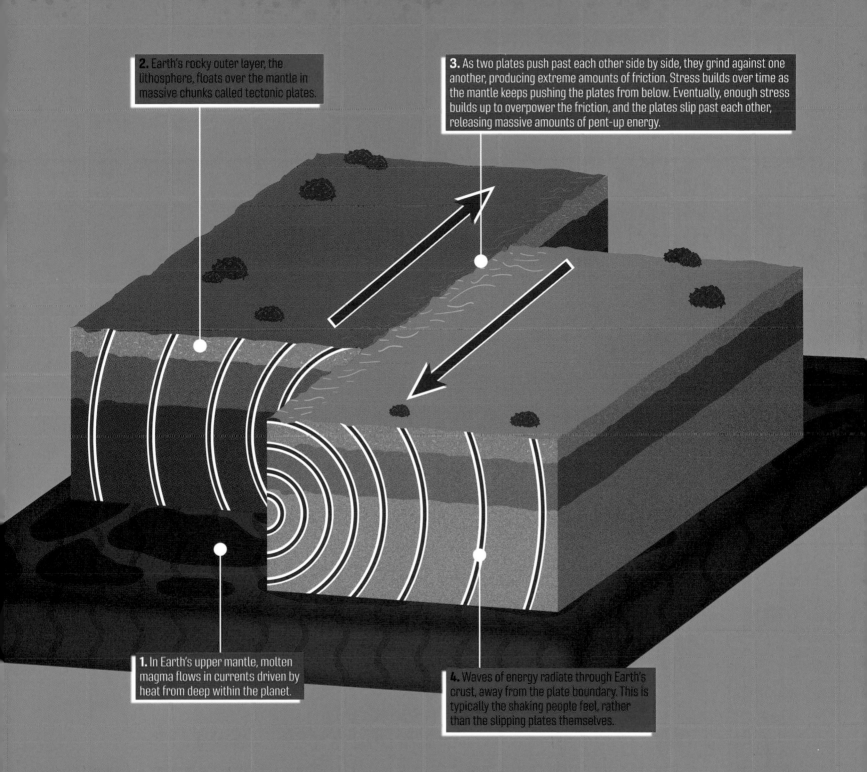

2. Earth's rocky outer layer, the lithosphere, floats over the mantle in massive chunks called tectonic plates.

3. As two plates push past each other side by side, they grind against one another, producing extreme amounts of friction. Stress builds over time as the mantle keeps pushing the plates from below. Eventually, enough stress builds up to overpower the friction, and the plates slip past each other, releasing massive amounts of pent-up energy.

1. In Earth's upper mantle, molten magma flows in currents driven by heat from deep within the planet.

4. Waves of energy radiate through Earth's crust, away from the plate boundary. This is typically the shaking people feel, rather than the slipping plates themselves.

FUN FACT >>> Every year there are about 500,000 EARTHQUAKES worldwide that INSTRUMENTS can detect, 100,000 that people can feel, and 100 THAT CAUSE DAMAGE.

TELL ME MORE

THE BIG GRIND

Lots of large-scale forces are at play in an earthquake. A big one is friction—the resistance to movement when things rub against each other. Try rubbing your hands together. Now push your palms toward each other as hard as you can and try rubbing them again. Do you feel the skin of one hand catching on the other and then suddenly lurching forward? That's basically what's happening as tectonic plates try to move past one another. The rocky plates grinding against each other create friction that keeps them from moving too far—until the pent-up pressure becomes too great. Then it overpowers the friction, releasing the plates from each other's grip and resulting in an earthquake. In some places, faults release stress in frequent small bursts, creating many minor quakes. In others, friction can keep the force building for hundreds of years before it finally lets go in one gigantic event.

The San Andreas Fault in California

FUN FACTS

>>> The **LARGEST EARTHQUAKE** ever recorded struck **CHILE** in 1960. It lasted for 10 minutes and clocked in at a magnitude of **9.5**, releasing more total energy than **130,000 NUCLEAR BOMBS.**

>>> The **MOON** also has earthquakes— er, moonquakes?—but they're **SMALLER AND LESS FREQUENT** than those on Earth.

>>> Southern California alone has about **10,000** earthquakes every year, but most of them are **TOO SMALL** to feel.

>>> The oldest **HISTORICAL EVIDENCE** of an earthquake dates back to **1831 B.C.,** when Chinese scholars noted the mountain **TAISHAN** wobbling in a quake.

TRY THIS!

How does friction affect the shaking in an earthquake? Lay two pieces of notebook paper one on top of the other and build a small tower of blocks on top. Gently pull the top piece of paper. Can you keep the tower standing? Now place two pieces of sandpaper on top of each other on the table so that the sand sides are facing one another. Build the same tower on top, then try to move the top paper. How does having more friction affect the tower?

FAULT LINES

A single plate boundary can create multiple faults, or cracks in Earth's crust along which earthquakes happen.

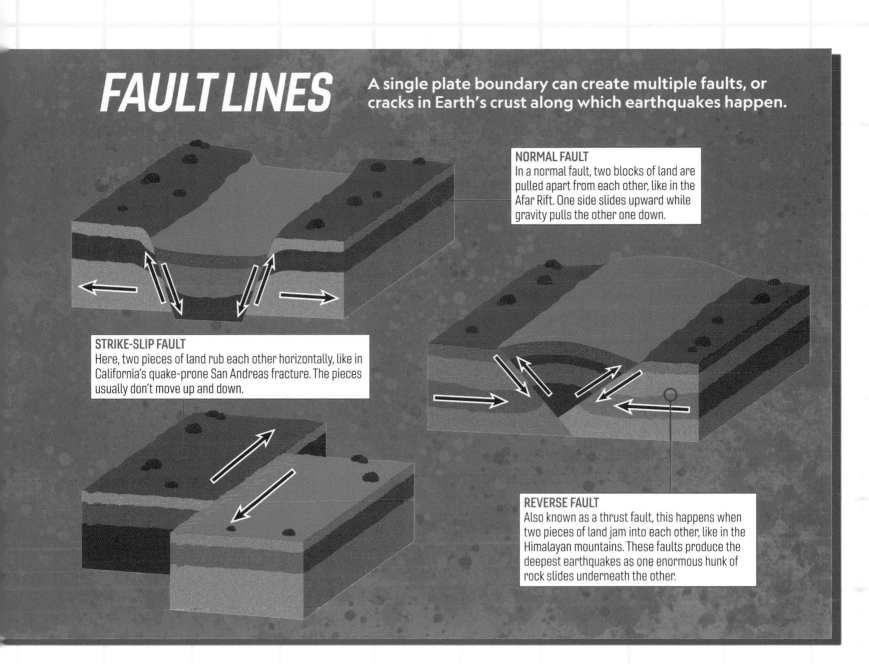

NORMAL FAULT
In a normal fault, two blocks of land are pulled apart from each other, like in the Afar Rift. One side slides upward while gravity pulls the other one down.

STRIKE-SLIP FAULT
Here, two pieces of land rub each other horizontally, like in California's quake-prone San Andreas fracture. The pieces usually don't move up and down.

REVERSE FAULT
Also known as a thrust fault, this happens when two pieces of land jam into each other, like in the Himalayan mountains. These faults produce the deepest earthquakes as one enormous hunk of rock slides underneath the other.

PUTTING IT BACK TOGETHER

We can't do anything to stop earthquakes. But we can be smart about how we build structures to increase their odds of surviving a big shake. In the 15th century, the Inca people built Machu Picchu in Peru between two fault lines in the mountains. It experiences frequent strong earthquakes, which could easily topple a stone structure. But the Inca outwitted this problem by choosing not to use mortar, the heavy paste that usually fills the gaps between building stones. Instead, they used precisely cut rocks that fit together like puzzle pieces. When an earthquake hits, the stones rattle, then easily fall back into place. Where rigid walls would have crumbled, the Incas' innovation helped keep their sprawling structure standing—and large parts of it have lasted to this day.

The ancient city of Machu Picchu

LESSON LEARNED!

ONE BIG QUAKE
OCTOBER 17, 1989

The Incident

It was a big day for baseball fans in Northern California. Two of their teams were in the World Series, and the third game was about to start. More than 60,000 people had packed into the bleachers at Candlestick Park in San Francisco, and the players were warming up on the field. Sportscasters at the stadium were introducing the big game on TV.

Then, out of nowhere, the stadium started shaking. Players felt queasy as the ground moved beneath their feet. Cracks formed in the upper decks of the park. As one of the sportscasters realized what was happening, he announced it on television: "I'll tell you what, we're having an earth—" And then the signal cut out.

The Loma Prieta earthquake measured 6.9 in magnitude. Everyone escaped the stadium safely, but the damage in other parts of the region was much worse. Roads fell apart, fires broke out, and some buildings collapsed entirely. All in all, 63 people died, more than 3,000 were injured, and about $6 billion worth of property was damaged.

What Went Wrong

Though the earthquake originated 60 miles (97 km) away from San Francisco, it did a lot of damage in the city. One of the worst-hit neighborhoods was the Marina District, built on former marshland. The soggy land had been filled in with rubble left from a previous earthquake in 1906. Then it was paved over, and roads and houses were built on top.

The problem? When loose, rocky, waterlogged ground starts shaking, it acts less like solid ground and more like a giant bowl of jelly. Waves of energy bounce back and forth and grow bigger, rocking whatever's on top more than the earthquake alone ever would. This phenomenon, which scientists call liquefaction, became extremely obvious as the sloshing soil toppled structures and tore apart underground utility pipes.

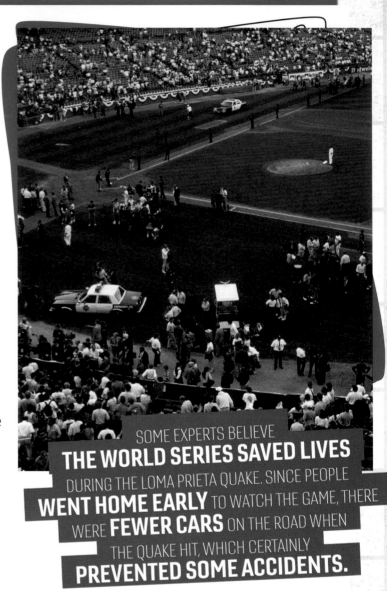

SOME EXPERTS BELIEVE **THE WORLD SERIES SAVED LIVES** DURING THE LOMA PRIETA QUAKE. SINCE PEOPLE **WENT HOME EARLY** TO WATCH THE GAME, THERE WERE **FEWER CARS** ON THE ROAD WHEN THE QUAKE HIT, WHICH CERTAINLY **PREVENTED SOME ACCIDENTS.**

THE BIG TAKEAWAY

SINCE THE LOMA PRIETA QUAKE, ENGINEERS AND CITY PLANNERS HAVE WORKED TO UNDERSTAND THE PROCESS OF LIQUEFACTION. In San Francisco and beyond, they've mapped areas with loose, rubbled ground that are most at risk in a big quake. They can build new buildings in these areas with strengthened designs to help them resist the stronger shaking. Expanding the underground foundations of existing buildings can also help prevent total collapse. Meanwhile, scientists are working on earthquake early-warning systems. These would detect quakes and alert people while they still have time to get to a safe spot.

FAKING QUAKES

ENGINEERS DON'T WANT TO WAIT FOR **EARTHQUAKES TO HAPPEN** TO FIGURE OUT HOW TO MAKE BUILDINGS STRONGER. SO HOW DO YOU **TEST** AN EARTHQUAKE WITHOUT DOING ANY **REAL DAMAGE?**

PLACE: Miki, Japan

Towering test facilities allow engineers to simulate the effects of quakes on all kinds of structures. This research institute in earthquake-prone Japan has a moving platform in the floor that can shake a life-size model building up to seven stories tall. After the test, engineers examine how the structure held up and discover its weak spots.

PLACE: San Diego, California, U.S.A.

The world's largest outdoor earthquake simulator is in Southern California at the University of California San Diego (UCSD). Since the Loma Prieta earthquake, thousands of buildings in San Francisco have been retrofitted, meaning they have been reinforced to make them safer. The earthquake simulator (called a shake table) at UCSD helped test these types of upgrades on actual full-size buildings to make sure they really did make structures safer.

CAN ANIMALS REALLY PREDICT EARTHQUAKES?
NO, BUT THEY CAN OFTEN **DETECT** THEM BEFORE HUMANS CAN. SOME ANIMALS FEEL THE **FAINTEST EARLY SHAKING** AND REACT BEFORE PEOPLE KNOW ANYTHING IS WRONG.

133

GONE TO ROT

How do formerly LIVING THINGS break down?

Want to see a magic trick? Step right up, and watch nature make a giant whale *disappear!* With the help of some bone-eating "zombie" worms, of course. (Wait, what?) To keep our big and complex planet running, formerly living things have to fall apart too. It can be a creepy, stinky, slimy spectacle—but it's also a really important one. Let's dive right in, but fair warning: This section isn't for the squeamish.

What is decomp-osition **?**

How does it happen **?**

Can it be stopped **?**

JUST THE FACTS

Breakdown Basics

It's a fundamental fact of life: Eventually, plants and animals stop living. And then, over time, the materials that make them up are broken down and recycled back into the ecosystem. Exactly how something decomposes depends on where it's located. In a warm, moist jungle where fungi and bacteria thrive, dead things break down faster than in the cold, dry Arctic. (Similarly, a banana left on the counter in summer rots faster than in the freezer.) But the basic process is always the same: The building blocks that make up the once living organism are taken apart and reused by other living things—many of them so small we can't even see them.

Burial at Sea

Take this extra-large example: When a whale dies in the ocean, it sinks to the seafloor. Though the whale itself is no longer living, it's still packed full of proteins, fats, sugars, and other ingredients necessary for life. Within days, living organisms find the whale and begin picking it apart. Sure, the whale is decomposing—but for deep-sea fish, worms, and other organisms, it's a downright feast. One dead whale can feed thousands of seafloor animals for decades after it dies. Scientists call this breakdown buffet a "whale fall."

WHAT'S FOR LUNCH?

Dead things rot because living things are gradually breaking them down. Here are some of the species that help by making meals of the long gone.

Creepy-crawly flesh-eating beetles (officially called dermestids) eat the skin and muscle off decaying carcasses. This process is called "skeletonization"—get it?

The bones of dead animals are up to 90 percent of the bearded vulture's diet. The 15-pound (7-kg) bird swallows smaller chunks of bone whole, and drops larger ones onto rocks to break them into smaller pieces.

When large creatures like whales decompose on the seafloor, they become covered in what looks like a beautiful garden of pinkish-orange flowers. In fact, these so-called bone-eating snot flowers are actually marine worms that are busy feeding on the carcass. And the parts that look like fluffy petals? They're balls of mucus.

Fungi are some of Earth's most important decomposers. Most species of fungus—including mold and, yes, mushrooms you might eat—sprout up on rotting plants or animals, using the nutrients they find there to live and grow.

Single-celled bacteria also do a lot of the work of breaking things down after death. The microorganisms break down complex cells from dead material, turning them into gases and minerals (some of which are responsible for a rotting thing's smell).

THREE-COURSE MEAL

While it decomposes, a dead whale makes a habitat for many types of living things.
They show up in stages, feeding on different parts of the massive carcass over several decades.

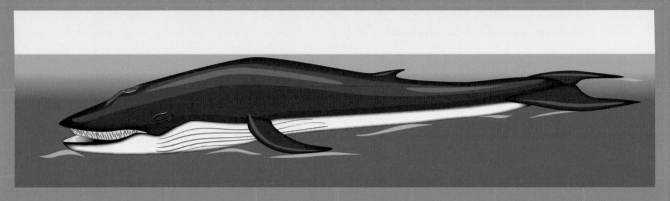

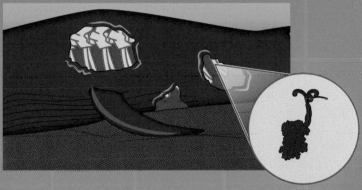

1. Within days of the dead whale sinking, scavengers sniff it out and swim over to tear off its muscle and blubber. Hagfish, sleeper sharks, and shrimplike amphipods work together to eat 90 to 130 pounds (40 to 60 kg) of flesh per day!

2. Within a year, smaller scavengers arrive to eat any remaining scraps of flesh, as well as energy-rich whale oil that has seeped onto the seafloor. As the skeleton is revealed, "zombie" worms—also known as bone-eating snot-flowers—latch on to eat the fats and oils inside.

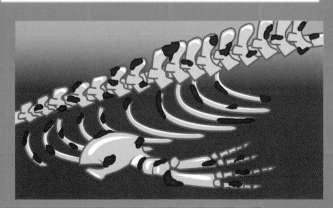

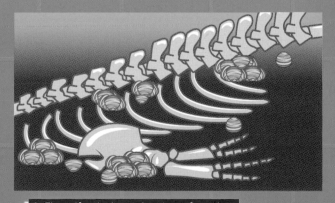

3. A year or two after the whale dies, thick mats of bacteria swarm the skeleton, breaking down what's left of the bones. This stage can last for decades until the skeleton completely disappears.

4. The sulfur the bacteria release from the bones attracts other animals, like deep-sea mussels and clams, that can get energy from the sulfur.

FUN FACT ⟩⟩ A single WHALE FALL can be home to nearly 200 different species—and that's not even counting BACTERIA and other microscopic CREEPY-CRAWLIES.

TELL ME MORE

BREAK IT UP

When you watch it happening, decomposition can seem gross. (Have you ever opened a container of food from the back of the fridge and found it full of stinky mold? Ew.) But decomposition is just a series of chemical reactions that break down dead material into smaller and smaller parts. Bigger scavengers break a dead plant or animal into smaller pieces to swallow. In their stomachs, enzymes (substances that speed up chemical reactions) act like tiny snippers, breaking big molecules apart into more digestible bits. Fungi and microscopic bacteria don't have stomachs, so they secrete enzymes onto the thing they're decomposing. The enzymes cut complicated molecules into smaller sugars that the fungi and bacteria can eat, plus nutrients like carbon and nitrogen that other living things need.

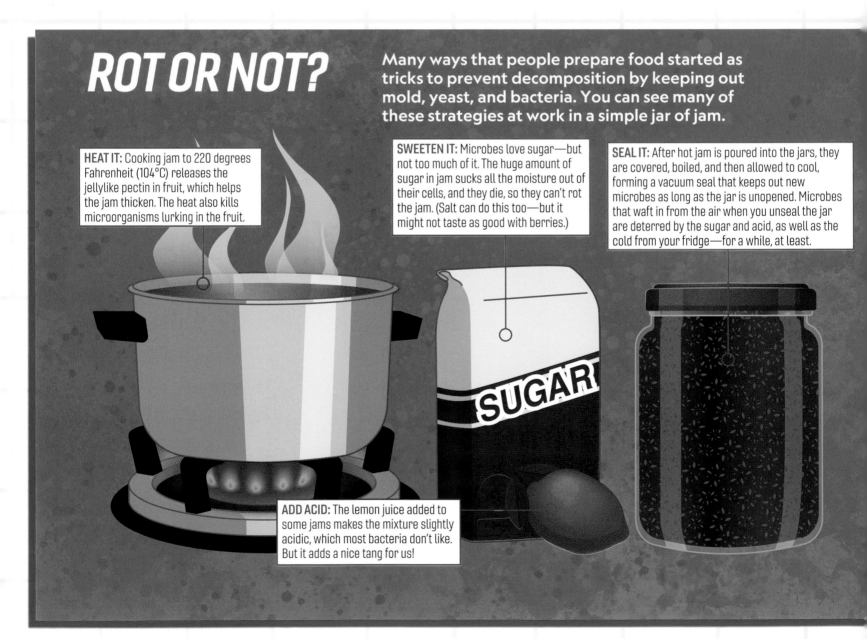

ROT OR NOT?

Many ways that people prepare food started as tricks to prevent decomposition by keeping out mold, yeast, and bacteria. You can see many of these strategies at work in a simple jar of jam.

HEAT IT: Cooking jam to 220 degrees Fahrenheit (104°C) releases the jellylike pectin in fruit, which helps the jam thicken. The heat also kills microorganisms lurking in the fruit.

SWEETEN IT: Microbes love sugar—but not too much of it. The huge amount of sugar in jam sucks all the moisture out of their cells, and they die, so they can't rot the jam. (Salt can do this too—but it might not taste as good with berries.)

SEAL IT: After hot jam is poured into the jars, they are covered, boiled, and then allowed to cool, forming a vacuum seal that keeps out new microbes as long as the jar is unopened. Microbes that waft in from the air when you unseal the jar are deterred by the sugar and acid, as well as the cold from your fridge—for a while, at least.

ADD ACID: The lemon juice added to some jams makes the mixture slightly acidic, which most bacteria don't like. But it adds a nice tang for us!

FUN FACTS

>>> Given enough time, **BACTERIA AND FUNGI** will eventually decompose anything that was once living—including cardboard, cotton, and **LEATHER CLOTHING.**

>>> There are **MORE MICROBES** in one **TEASPOON OF SOIL** than there are **PEOPLE ON EARTH!**

>>> One **YEAST SPECIES** that decomposes food releases stinky sulfur compounds similar to those in **HUMAN FARTS.**

>>> The Arctic tundra sometimes naturally **FREEZE-DRIES** bodies. In 2007, a **HERDER** in Siberia discovered a perfectly preserved **BABY MAMMOTH** that had been frozen in place for **40,000 YEARS.**

Yeast granules are dormant when dry, but will wake up when added to warm water.

IT'S KIND OF A FUNNY STORY ...

Remember that dead whale? They usually sink out of sight. But sometimes they wash up and start decomposing on shore, which can cause some whale-size problems. In November 1970, a dead whale drifted onto a beach in Oregon, U.S.A. After three days, the stench had become unbearable, and engineers were brought in to figure out how to get rid of the rotting behemoth. They decided to blast the whale to smithereens and let seagulls and other scavengers clean up the resulting scraps. What could possibly go wrong? The team packed the whale with dynamite and cleared the area a quarter mile (400 m) around. But as soon as they pushed the plunger, their plan backfired—literally. Bits of whale flew farther than expected, in just about every direction. Chunks of blubber dented cars and rained down on innocent bystanders. No one was hurt in the incident—just unbelievably grossed out.

AVALAAAAAANCHE!

How does a MOUNTAINSIDE of snow suddenly collapse?

It's a quiet day in the mountains. The air is brisk, and the midday sun is reflecting off a deep layer of bright white snow. Suddenly you hear a rumble above you, and you look up to see a wall of snow speeding down the mountain. The odds of outrunning it are slim—maybe even impossible. This is what it's like to experience an avalanche, and not everyone who does makes it out alive. How do avalanches do their damage, and why do they form in some conditions and not others? Bundle up: It's going to get chilly in here.

Why do avalanches happen **?**

What makes them so dangerous **?**

How can they be avoided **?**

Sweet powder, bro!

JUST THE FACTS

Scary Snow

An untouched blanket of deep, powdery snow is a tempting vision to outdoor thrill seekers. Where some of us see a reason to stay inside with hot chocolate, mountain climbers, snowmobilers, and backcountry skiers see adventure waiting. But at the top of their mind—if they're being sensible, that is—is the risk of triggering an avalanche. These seriously dangerous snowslides can turn a day in a winter wonderland into a fight for survival.

Avalanche Ingredients

Avalanches don't form just anywhere. First, snow has to build up on a mountainside of the right steepness—typically an angle between 30 and 50 degrees. If it's steeper than that, snow probably won't collect in large enough amounts. Less steep, and snow is unlikely to start moving down the slope. Once snow has built up, something has to trigger it to loosen and start flowing downward. Anything that weakens the snowpack, or vibrates it once it's already weak, can set an avalanche in motion—like a change in weather, the rumble from a passing snowmobiler, the pressure from a downhill skier, or the crash of a falling tree.

SLIDING STYLES

Avalanches can form in many different ways, but here are three major types—from least to most dangerous.

LOOSE-SNOW AVALANCHE: This powdery snowslide, also called a sluff, forms when loose, new fallen snow rolls off a slope too steep to support it. A loose-snow avalanche typically starts from a single point, then fans outward as it gains more snow and cascades down the slope.

ICE AVALANCHE: This form of avalanche happens when pieces of a glacier—a large, slow-moving mass of ice—flow over the edge of a rock face. As blocks of ice fall, they might begin to slide and collect snow with them, or trigger a separate slab avalanche.

SLAB AVALANCHE: The most dangerous and unpredictable type of avalanche occurs when heavy snow builds up on top of a weaker layer buried beneath it. If the weak layer breaks apart, the top layer slides down the mountain in an enormous slab, breaking into massive chunks on the way down.

SLAB OF DESTRUCTION

Slab avalanches are the most common—and most deadly—form of snowslide in the mountains.

Starting zone: Most avalanches begin on a high-up slope, where an unstable layer of snow is covered by heavier snow. The unstable snow shifts, causing the upper slab to start sliding downhill. It can reach a speed of 20 miles an hour (30 km/h) within about three seconds.

Avalanche track: The sliding snow quickly accelerates to up to 80 miles an hour (130 km/h) as it races down through the mountains. As it flows downhill, it can break into chunks weighing many tons each, knocking down trees and anything else in its path.

Runout zone: At or near the bottom of the slope, the snow and any debris it has collected pile up in a massive, solid heap. This is where people are most likely to be caught in the avalanche.

FUN FACT >>> A LARGE AVALANCHE can contain 300,000 cubic yards (230,000 m³) of snow—enough to pile 20 FOOTBALL FIELDS 10 feet (3 m) deep.

FUN FACT >>> Some SKI RESORTS drop dynamite from helicopters to set off INTENTIONAL SMALL AVALANCHES, clearing unstable snow layers before SKIERS show up for the season.

TELL ME MORE

FREEZING FRICTION

The difference between a weak snow layer and stable one depends a lot on the type of snowflakes within it. One reason is our old friend friction. The shape, size, temperature, arrangement, and melting-and-freezing history of snowflakes all affect how much friction they have with each other—or how long they can cling together without breaking apart. The classic branching snowflakes tangle together easily, like jigsaw-puzzle pieces in a box. But small, icy particles can act more like a pile of marbles. They might still be able to stay stacked at first, but one wrong move will break them apart, sending the more stable layers above them tumbling down in a heap.

>>> Can **YELLING TOO LOUD** really trigger an avalanche, like in the movies? **SCIENTISTS SAY NO**—the vibrations from your voice aren't nearly strong enough, no matter **HOW LOUD** you shout.

>>> The power of a **SLAB AVALANCHE** can move a **WHOLE BUILDING** and carry objects— **OR PEOPLE**—hundreds of feet down a slope.

>>> The **SWISS ALPS** have an average of **80,000 AVALANCHES** every year.

The Swiss Alps are beautiful—and prone to avalanches.

TRY THIS!

Look out below! Make your own avalanche with a couple of heavy hardcover books and a layer of salt. Stack one heavy book on top of another. Slowly lift the edge of the bottom book until the top book slides off. Now sprinkle salt on the bottom book before placing the other on top. Lift the edge of the bottom book again and see if the top book slides off faster. In a slab avalanche, a loose layer of snow shifts, causing the heavy layer on top to dislodge and begin to slide quickly—just like the top book slides off the salt.

SNOWPACK STYLES

One way experts analyze avalanche risk is by digging a hole and examining the layers of snowpack inside it, like looking at the layers in a cake.

STABLE SNOW

UNSTABLE SNOW

Pointed snowflakes with frozen water droplets on their surface cling together to form a thick slab.

SOFT, FRESH SNOW

OLDER, PACKED-DOWN SNOW

GROUND

RECENT SNOW PACKED DOWN BY WIND

LOOSE OR GRAINY LAYER

OLDER, PACKED-DOWN SNOW

GROUND

When it's extremely cold, water vapor from the air can freeze directly into grainy ice crystals on the snow surface. These don't hold together well once new snow falls on top.

AVALANCHE RISK: LOW

AVALANCHE RISK: HIGH

HOW THINGS WORKED

In the late 17th century, Swiss monks living in the Alps started using Saint Bernard dogs to rescue travelers who'd been trapped by avalanches and other incidents. With their keen sense of smell, the dogs could sniff out lost or buried victims and lead rescuers to them. Rescue dogs (of many breeds) are still used by avalanche response teams around the world. So are long metal probes that help rescuers search through the snow, and so are beacons, small devices worn by backcountry explorers that send out a signal if they're trapped in an avalanche. These all serve the same purpose: to lead rescuers to an avalanche victim as quickly as possible, increasing the odds that the person will survive.

We've Got a Job to Do

STORM CHASER

Tornadoes are some of nature's most powerful agents of destruction. Their furious funnel-shaped winds can reach more than 200 miles an hour (322 km/h), uprooting trees, tearing off roofs, and flattening entire homes. "Tornadoes are the single most intense windstorm on the planet," says Robin Tanamachi, a meteorologist at Purdue University in Indiana, U.S.A. She's trying to learn more about these powerful storms to better predict where and how they'll do their worst.

" MOTHER NATURE HOLDS ALL THE CARDS. "

Most of the time, Tanamachi crunches data and writes scientific papers. But during tornado season in the U.S.—from about April to July—she heads to places like Tornado Alley, the windy stretch of land between Nebraska and Texas where tornadoes often form. She and her colleagues pile into a truck with laptops, video cameras, and scientific equipment. They chase down the spots where the biggest and most powerful storms are brewing, sometimes driving more than 600 miles (966 km).

They're looking for supercells—giant, rotating thunderstorms that can form where cold air overlies warm air and stretch more than 10 miles (16 km) across. The strong, spiraling winds in these storms make them the most likely to spew out tornadoes. When Tanamachi's team finds a supercell, they park at what they hope is a safe distance from it. They set up a radar scanner, which sends out beams of electromagnetic energy to detect wind speeds inside the swirling storm.

Tanamachi stays as safe as she can, but she has had close calls. In 2013, a massive tornado she was observing in El Reno, Oklahoma, changed direction suddenly—and she realized it was coming straight at her. "That was the only time I've ever felt afraid of being overtaken by a tornado," she says. "Within five seconds, everybody was back in the car, buckled in, and we were racing back home. That experience reminded me that Mother Nature holds all the cards."

But collecting data from tornadoes could help change that. Understanding how the storms form helps Tanamachi build computer models that simulate them. That could eventually help scientists predict when and where tornadoes are most likely to appear. This could give people more time to get away from an oncoming twister—and reduce the number of false alarms.

ROBIN TANAMACHI BECAME INTERESTED IN **SEVERE WEATHER** AS A KID, WHEN SHE SAW A **NEWS REPORT** ABOUT AN **ACTIVE TORNADO** LIVE ON TV.

THE TORNADO IN EL RENO REACHED **2.6 MILES** (4.2 KM) ACROSS—THE **LARGEST** SCIENTISTS HAVE EVER RECORDED **ON EARTH.**

THE AVERAGE TIME BETWEEN A **TORNADO WARNING** AND WHEN IT **STRIKES** IS **13 MINUTES.**

Tornado Damage

How destructive is a tornado? That depends on how fast its swirling winds blow.

65–85 miles an hour (105–137 km/h)

Shingles are blown off houses and branches break off trees.

86–110 miles an hour (138–177 km/h)

Windows break and doors fly off their hinges.

111–135 miles an hour (178–217 km/h)

Roofs can be torn off completely, and trees are pulled up from their roots.

136–165 miles an hour (219–266 km/h)

Homes can lose entire stories as wind tears them apart.

166–200 miles an hour (267–322 km/h)

Well-built houses are completely flattened, and cars fly through the air.

More than 200 miles an hour (322 km/h)

Homes are completely swept away, concrete buildings crack, and entire trees are completely torn to pieces.

PLAGUE OF PESTS

How does one SWARM of insects destroy miles and miles of crops?

Imagine you're minding your own business on your front porch. Suddenly the sky darkens, and you hear an eerie buzzing. You look up and see a huge dark cloud. No, wait—it's a flying mass of millions of insects, and they stretch as far as the eye can see. Locusts! These swarming insects have been a pest on crops since ancient times, but what's the real deal with these legendary bugs? You might want to keep your eyes and mouth covered, because we're heading into a swarm.

What are locusts **?**

Why do they form swarms **?**

How much damage can they do **?**

149

JUST THE FACTS

Super Swarms

Locusts are a type of grasshopper. But while most grasshoppers are harmless, locusts are some of the world's most devastating pests. That's because they have a particularly nasty superpower. They're typically solitary insects—meaning they live alone. But under the right conditions, they form giant, hungry, migrating swarms that devour every plant in their path. These swarms are called plagues, and that's not an exaggeration. The migrating swarms can stretch across the sky and fly up to 93 miles (150 km) each day, leaving the land barren of crops in their wake.

Making of a Plague

Locust swarms can emerge in parts of Africa, Asia, the Middle East, and Australia. These areas all have desert land that very rarely gets heavy rain. Before the rains, the locust population is small. The bugs feed on the sparse patches of vegetation and stay out of each other's way. When it does rain heavily after a long drought, the dry landscape changes. Plants temporarily pop up, allowing those few locusts to eat a lot—and breed a lot too. But sometimes the rains die down by the time their eggs hatch, and there aren't enough plants to feed all the individuals in the new generation of locusts. So the young insects crowd together in the few remaining green areas. But being around so many other locusts triggers their bodies to release a chemical that changes their behavior. Instead of avoiding each other, they form a swarm that then takes flight in search of new sources of food.

WHAT'S THE DIFFERENCE?

In North America, the word "locust" is sometimes used to refer to other bugs. But these insects aren't true locusts of the plaguing kind.

GRASSHOPPERS are a large group of jumping insects that live in habitats around the world. There are thousands of species that don't typically migrate or form swarms.

CICADAS are bugs that hatch in large numbers after resting underground for up to 17 years. These sudden swarms remind people of locusts, but cicadas aren't closely related.

LOCUSTS are a particular type of grasshopper—the only type that forms ravenous swarms. They migrate much farther than regular grasshoppers and are far more destructive than cicadas.

FUN FACT »» An adult locust can EAT ITS OWN WEIGHT in vegetation every day. That's like an average adult human eating more than 400 CHEESEBURGERS every 24 hours.

FORMING A SWARM

Desert locusts are the most destructive locust species. Here's how they turn from loner insects into a mass of crop killers.

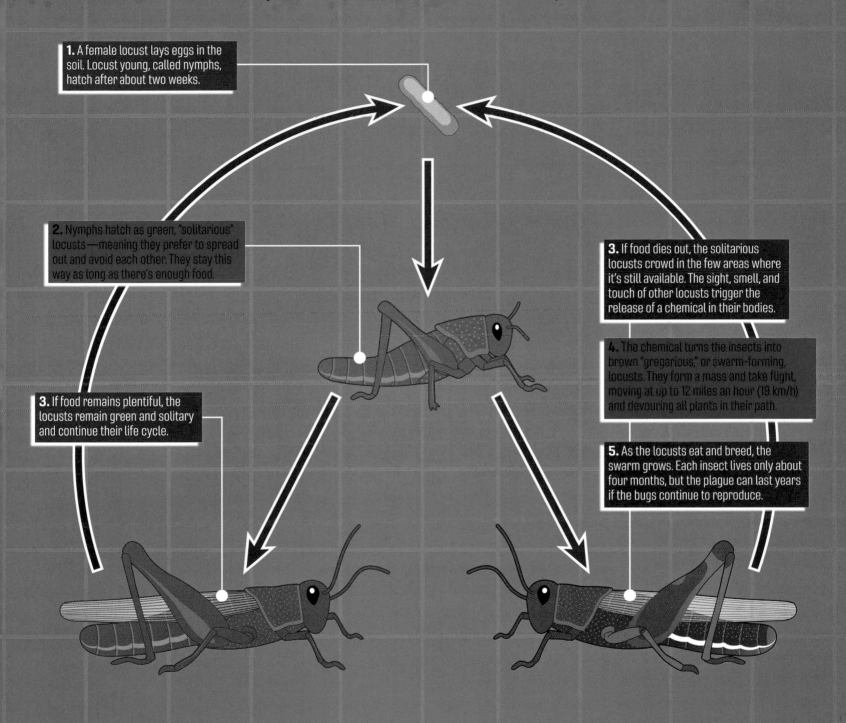

1. A female locust lays eggs in the soil. Locust young, called nymphs, hatch after about two weeks.

2. Nymphs hatch as green, "solitarious" locusts—meaning they prefer to spread out and avoid each other. They stay this way as long as there's enough food.

3. If food remains plentiful, the locusts remain green and solitary and continue their life cycle.

3. If food dies out, the solitarious locusts crowd in the few areas where it's still available. The sight, smell, and touch of other locusts trigger the release of a chemical in their bodies.

4. The chemical turns the insects into brown "gregarious," or swarm-forming, locusts. They form a mass and take flight, moving at up to 12 miles an hour (19 km/h) and devouring all plants in their path.

5. As the locusts eat and breed, the swarm grows. Each insect lives only about four months, but the plague can last years if the bugs continue to reproduce.

FUN FACT >>> Desert locusts can invade up to ONE-FIFTH of the land on EARTH during years when they form swarms.

TELL ME MORE

EAT OR BE EATEN

Locusts don't start swarming because they feel friendly. They do it because they're hungry—so hungry that even their fellow locusts look like a good snack. When the insects crowd together, they start trying to chase each other. But each one is also trying to avoid all the other locusts chasing it. As millions of bugs all try to hunt and escape being hunted, they form a giant moving mass. It's like one enormous game of tag where everyone is "it." The result is that the swarm acts less like a bunch of individuals and more like a mass of flowing liquid. It pours across the landscape, eating anything green in its path.

GROUP DYNAMICS

Scientists have found that the motion of a group of locusts depends on how densely they're packed together.

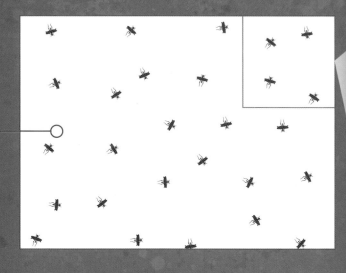

SOLITARIOUS LOCUSTS spread out as much as possible to avoid each other. This motion is similar to the particles in a gas spreading out.

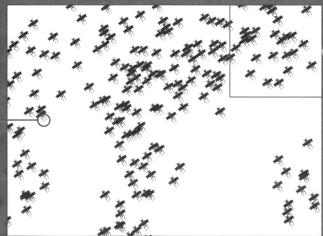

GREGARIOUS LOCUSTS start moving in the same direction as they try to eat each other but avoid being eaten. This keeps them close together but constantly moving, like a flowing liquid.

FUN FACTS

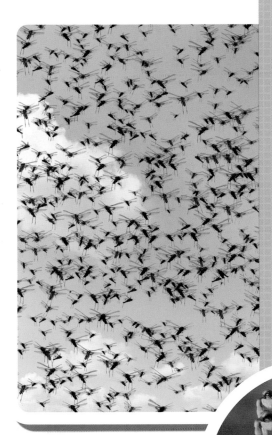

Dry-fried locusts ready for snacking

>>> The **1875 ROCKY MOUNTAIN** locust swarm may have contained up to **3.5 TRILLION LOCUSTS**—more than **450 TIMES** the current human population of Earth!

>>> Some experts have suggested dealing with **LOCUST POPULATIONS** by **SNACKING** on the bugs.

>>> Locusts look so different in their **SOLITARY** and **SWARMING** forms that scientists thought they were **TWO DIFFERENT SPECIES** until 1921.

>>> Scientists have **TRICKED LOCUSTS** into changing into their swarming form by **TICKLING** their back legs to make them feel as if they're **IN A CROWD.**

The bodies of swarming locusts have a spotted pattern.

HOW THINGS WORKED

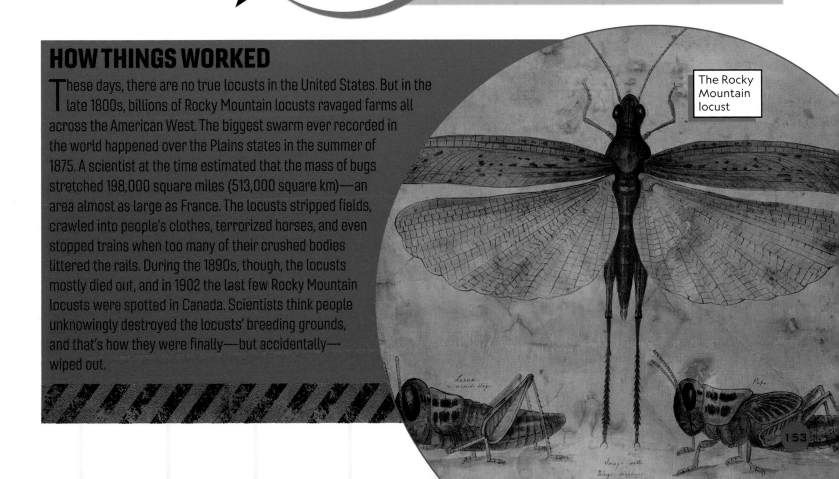

These days, there are no true locusts in the United States. But in the late 1800s, billions of Rocky Mountain locusts ravaged farms all across the American West. The biggest swarm ever recorded in the world happened over the Plains states in the summer of 1875. A scientist at the time estimated that the mass of bugs stretched 198,000 square miles (513,000 square km)—an area almost as large as France. The locusts stripped fields, crawled into people's clothes, terrorized horses, and even stopped trains when too many of their crushed bodies littered the rails. During the 1890s, though, the locusts mostly died out, and in 1902 the last few Rocky Mountain locusts were spotted in Canada. Scientists think people unknowingly destroyed the locusts' breeding grounds, and that's how they were finally—but accidentally—wiped out.

The Rocky Mountain locust

TRY THIS!

APPLE MUMMIES

KEEP APPLES FROM DECOMPOSING

The ancient Egyptians kept human bodies from decomposing by turning them into mummies. They used natron—a natural substance mined from lake beds—to preserve the bodies by drying them out. You can mimic this process by making "mummies" out of apples. Creepy *and* scientific!

WHAT YOU NEED

TIME: 30 to 60 minutes—and a week of waiting

1. An adult to help with peeling and carving

2. 4 apples

3. Vegetable peeler

4. Mixing bowl

5. Spoon

6. About 1 cup (273 g)* salt

7. About 1 cup (180 g)* baking soda

8. About 2 cups (400 g)* sugar

9. About 2 cups (370 g)* uncooked rice

10. 4 clean plastic containers with lids from the recycling, big enough to fit an apple with some room to spare (ideally all the same size)

11. Marker

12. Craft stick or plastic pumpkin-carving tools (optional)

* Depending on the size of your apples and plastic container. You may want to keep extra on hand in case you need more.

WHAT TO DO

1. Ask an adult to peel the apples. It's OK if some bits of peel are left—you just need most of the fruit to be exposed.

2. If you'd like, ask an adult to help carve a face in each apple using the craft stick or pumpkin-carving tools. Make the eye and mouth holes pretty deep. (This step is optional but will make the end result way more fun.)

3. In the mixing bowl, mix the salt and baking soda together and stir well.

4. Place one apple in each plastic container. Completely cover one apple with the uncooked rice, one apple with sugar, and one apple with the salt and baking soda mixture. Leave the last apple uncovered. Put lids on the containers.

5. Use the marker to label each container with the preservative you used.

6. Place the apple containers out of the way and leave them untouched for about a week. Then unbury the apples and examine them next to the unpreserved one. How do they look? Which preservative worked best?

WARNING: Don't eat the apple mummies or the preservatives! (Don't eat the rotted apple either—but you knew that, right?)

WHAT TO EXPECT

The untreated apple should get pretty gross. But at least some of the others will fare better. A well-preserved apple should feel drier and lighter than it was originally. If you carved a face, check how recognizable it still is.

WHAT'S GOING ON?

Natron is a great desiccant—a substance that dries things out by absorbing water. Without moisture, mold and bacteria have a much harder time doing their job of decomposing things that were once alive. Salt, baking soda, sugar, and rice are all desiccants of different strengths. How well they preserve your apple depends on how much moisture they soak up.

CHAPTER 5

EVERYDAY CHAOS

Giant explosions are pretty awe inspiring.
BUT HOW OFTEN DO YOU GET TO WITNESS THE FORCES OF DESTRUCTION IN YOUR DAY-TO-DAY LIFE?

All the time, actually—if you know where to look. Many of the same forces that take apart buildings and mountainsides are at work when a balloon pops, a phone screen shatters, or a bicycle left outside starts to rust. Of course, you really shouldn't destroy things on purpose (seriously, don't try this at home). But understanding how these things break can help you keep them whole, so let's get to it!

THE BIG BURST

How does a balloon POP?

Ah, balloons, those perfect party decorations. Whether they're bobbing on a string or hanging out in a colorful bunch, they're tons of fun. But one wrong move, and—POP! That balloon is done forever. What happened to turn that air-filled bubble of joy into a useless scrap of rubber? Well, we're about to find out—so you might want to cover your ears.

What are balloons made of ?

How do they inflate ?

What happens when they pop ?

JUST THE FACTS

Preparing to Pop

Most of the colorful balloons you see at parties are made of a thin sheet of latex, a form of rubber that originally comes from plants. Latex's special talent is its elasticity—the ability to stretch a serious amount without breaking. As you blow up a balloon, its latex skin stretches thinner and thinner. But this stretching creates tension in the balloon as the material tries to pull itself back to its original state. Meanwhile, the air or helium inside the balloon wants to expand outward—but the balloon skin won't let it. As the gas and the latex push against each other, they create a high-pressure situation that primes the balloon to pop.

Breaking Free

The fuller a balloon is, the more tightly the latex is stretched all around it. Every molecule in the stretchy material is pulling on every molecule around it. With enough of this tension built up, all it takes is a slight prick from something sharp—or a tiny rip as one part of the balloon stretches too far—to break the molecules apart and start the popping process. As soon as there's a break in the balloon skin, the tension releases in that one spot, followed by the areas around it. At the same time, the pressurized air or helium from inside the balloon bursts out of its new escape hatch. It expands rapidly into the air around it, creating a tiny shock wave that you hear as the balloon's "pop."

INSTANT EXPLOSION

It takes only a fraction of a second for a balloon to pop— far too fast to see. Here's what's really happening.

Keep the party indoors, OK? Wildlife experts warn against releasing balloons outside, where animals can get hurt if they mistake the popped pieces for food.

1. Before a balloon pops, the pull on the skin is equal in all directions. The instant a hole forms, the tension breaks in that one spot.

2. Tension is still stretching the latex molecules in the rest of the balloon. But since the molecules around the edge of the hole no longer have anything to grab onto, they're pulled away from the hole, and the hole grows.

3. The contracting latex can move as fast as 1,870 feet per second (570 m/s)—almost twice the speed of sound. The gas rapidly expanding out of the balloon creates the popping noise.

4. The balloon skin keeps contracting until all the tension is released. It crumples into a point opposite from where it was pricked.

FUN FACT »»» Balloons can POP even if nothing touches them. GAS EXPANDS as it warms, so a balloon baking in the sun or the back of a hot car can stretch until it SUDDENLY BURSTS.

TELL ME MORE

STRETCHED TO BREAKING

What makes latex so good at stretching? The secret is at the microscopic level. Latex is made of long strings of molecules that are loosely joined together. This gives them room to spread apart while still remaining connected. Picture yourself and some friends holding hands in a circle. If you keep the circle small, your arms will dangle between you, and you'll still be able to move around. But start stepping back to make the circle bigger without letting go of each other's hands, and you'll start to feel your arms stretching out more and more. There's only so far you can all pull apart before the tension becomes too much and you have to let go of each other. Pop!

FUN FACTS

>>> Some of the **FIRST BALLOONS** are thought to have been made by the ancient **AZTEC.** They inflated tube-shaped animal **INTESTINES** and twisted them into "animal balloons" to offer to the gods as sacrifice.

>>> Weather balloons use **POPPING** to their advantage. They expand as they rise through Earth's **ATMOSPHERE,** then break open, sending the scientific equipment they carried back to **RESEARCHERS ON THE GROUND.**

TRY THIS!

Can you poke a balloon without a loud pop? Blow up a balloon and tie it off. Now put a piece of masking tape somewhere on the balloon. Use a thumbtack to poke through the tape. The balloon won't pop in a burst. It will deflate slowly. That's because the tape isn't under tension like the balloon skin. It's also stronger than the balloon beneath it.

Toby might be a balloon-popping champ, but you should never let your dog chomp on balloons—dogs can be seriously hurt if they accidentally swallow any part of a balloon.

IT'S KIND OF A FUNNY STORY ...

Many pets—and people—are startled by the sound of balloons popping. But Toby the whippet loves it. Once while on a walk, Toby found a balloon caught in a fence and quickly punctured it with his sharp teeth. He loved it. Toby's human, Christie Springs of Calgary, Canada, remembered seeing a video of a dog popping 100 balloons fast enough to set a world record. She figured Toby might have a shot at breaking it, so she started training him, even filling a pool with balloons and letting Toby swim around and grab them like a shark. Toby now holds the world record for dog balloon popping: 100 balloons in just 28.22 seconds. Beat that!

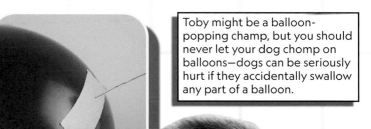

SCREEN SAVER

How does a SMARTPHONE screen shatter?

It almost happens in slow motion: Your phone slips from your hand, tumbles through the air, and lands on the pavement with a terrifying clatter. For a few seconds, you hold your breath. Did the screen crack? Did it miraculously survive the fall? How much of a beating is it designed to take, anyway? We're about to take a closer look at how tough these thin screens actually are—and what happens when the hit they take is even tougher. Are you charged up?

What is a phone screen made of ?

How does it resist cracking ?

What makes it break ?

JUST THE FACTS

Daily Grind

We don't have to tell you this, but smartphones are everywhere. More than three billion people around the world carry these devices around with them. Many people pick them up and look at them dozens of times every day. But this handling can make for a lot of wear and tear on the phones, which bump against things in bags, get squished in pockets, or even tumble onto the ground. The good news: Smartphone screens are specially designed to resist damage from these everyday accidents.

Tough as Glass

First, it's helpful to know how a tiny touchscreen is put together. The secret is layers of ultrathin glass, sandwiched together into a screen just a few millimeters thick. But the result isn't as fragile as you might expect, because of how it's made. First, workers mix sand with other substances and melt it in an ultrahot oven. The hot liquid flows out of the oven like a waterfall to form a thin glass sheet. As the glass cools in the air, it hardens. Robots pick it up by the edges, carefully cut it, and then bathe it in a chemical treatment that helps it resist damage.

BY THE NUMBERS

How big of a problem is phone-dropping? Check out some stats from the smartphone industry.

An estimated **85 percent** of smartphone owners drop their phones at least once a year.

In the U.S. alone, two smartphone screens break **every second**. (At least eight broke in the time it took you to read that sentence!)

About **49 percent** of cracked screens happen when the phone falls out of someone's pocket—and that doesn't include the ones that get sat on.

Americans spend **$3.4 billion** a year repairing cracked screens.

About **38 percent** of people with broken phone screens don't bother replacing them—they just keep using the phone, cracks and all.

FUN FACT ≫ Glass manufacturers can make screen layers as THIN as 100 microns—about as wide as A HUMAN HAIR. Several are SANDWICHED TOGETHER to make a screen.

LIGHT-UP LAYERS

A high-end phone touchscreen is made of multiple layers of glass,
each just a fraction of a millimeter thick.

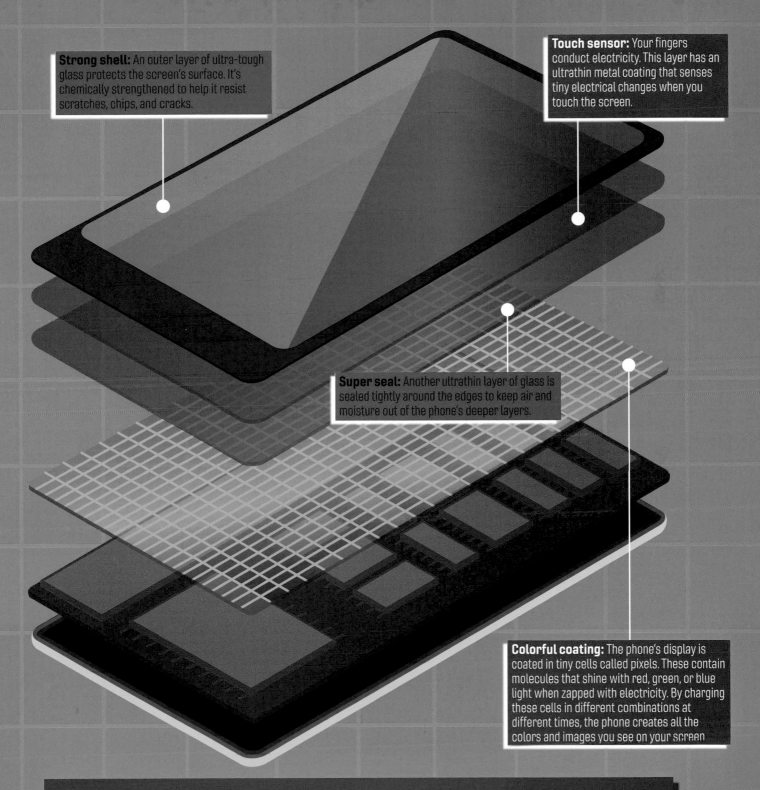

Strong shell: An outer layer of ultra-tough glass protects the screen's surface. It's chemically strengthened to help it resist scratches, chips, and cracks.

Touch sensor: Your fingers conduct electricity. This layer has an ultrathin metal coating that senses tiny electrical changes when you touch the screen.

Super seal: Another ultrathin layer of glass is sealed tightly around the edges to keep air and moisture out of the phone's deeper layers.

Colorful coating: The phone's display is coated in tiny cells called pixels. These contain molecules that shine with red, green, or blue light when zapped with electricity. By charging these cells in different combinations at different times, the phone creates all the colors and images you see on your screen.

FUN FACT >>> It's a sign of the times: The same New York company that made the glass for THOMAS EDISON'S first lightbulbs now makes glass for BILLIONS OF SMARTPHONES around the world.

Just like the safety glass in cars, glass for the outer layer of phone screens is tempered to strengthen it, but this time using a special chemical process rather than just heat. After a glass sheet is formed at the factory, it's dunked in a bath of hot, salty liquid. This liquid simmers at about 750 degrees Fahrenheit (400°C)—hot enough so that the tiny atoms that make up the glass bounce around a bit, but not hot enough to melt the material entirely. As the glass sits in the salt bath, atoms of potassium from the hot liquid seep into the glass's surface. They force out smaller atoms of sodium from the glass and wedge themselves into the sodium's old spots. As these bigger atoms squeeze into the glass, they push on the atoms next to them. This forms a layer of compression—or pressing force—that makes it harder for a piece of dirt to scratch through. The compression layer makes a screen strong enough to protect it if something hits it flat on its surface. But an impact from the wrong angle (say, dropping the phone on its corner) can release the energy of the squeezed-in atoms and shatter the thin glass.

FUN FACTS

>>> About **26 PERCENT** of damaged phones aren't cracked at all. They have a more **EMBARRASSING** problem: Their owners dropped them in the toilet!

>>> Sometimes **LONG FALLS** aren't a problem. In 2017, a man accidentally dropped his phone **1,000 FEET** (305 m) out of a small airplane and into a stranger's garden—and it **STILL WORKED FINE!**

>>> To make glass for phone screens, workers heat it to more than **1800 DEGREES** Fahrenheit (980°C)—as hot as freshly erupted **LAVA!**

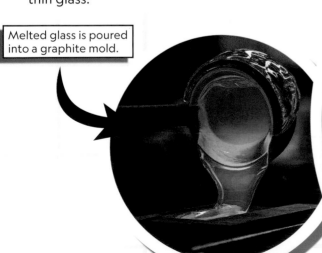

Melted glass is poured into a graphite mold.

FREE FALL

Is your phone's screen going to break when you drop your phone? That depends partly on the angle at which it hits.

When a screen lands flat, the force from hitting the ground presses flat against it. The strengthened compression layer pushes back, spreading out the force and reducing the impact on any one part of the glass.

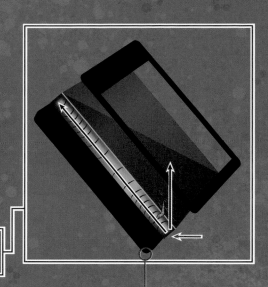

If a corner of the screen hits the ground, the force of the hit is concentrated in one place. This can create enough pressure to break through the compression layer, releasing the energy inside the glass and shattering the screen.

WHOA... SLOW DOWN.
A CLOSER LOOK AT COMPRESSION.

The forces of compression are complicated. To make things a little more transparent, let's do a thought experiment. Say you and a friend sit together on a two-person bus seat. If a third person squeezed in between you, you'd feel the push of compression as your bodies squished together tight. Now, if a fourth person tried to join, they'd have trouble—the three of you are so packed together that you're difficult to push through. OK, now pretend you and your friends are atoms in a piece of glass—that's the compressed layer of a phone screen. If a piece of grit tries to squeeze in and scratch it, it's pushed back out by the compressive force of the atoms in the glass. But a hard-enough hit can overpower the compression, releasing the pent-up energy inside the glass.

The atoms in a piece of glass

167

We've Got a Job to Do

How does everyday use cause the things we love to break? How can designers build them to stand up better to repeated wear and tear? Figuring this out is the job of test engineers like Tim Piumarta. He's the director of research and development at NHS Inc., a company in Santa Cruz, California. His lab smashes, scrapes, and sandblasts skateboards to find their weak spots and identify how they can be improved.

> ## "EVERY DAY I WALK IN AND SAY, 'OH BOY, WHAT ARE WE GOING TO LEARN TODAY?'"

Piumarta grew up skateboarding and building his own basic boards at home. "I had an incredibly strong curiosity to learn how things work and how to make them better," he says. As a teenager, he started test-riding skateboards for NHS, and he eventually landed a job there. He's now involved with every skateboard part the company designs.

Originally, Piumarta and his team tested skateboards on the street—just how people would use them. But it was time-consuming, and he couldn't always pinpoint what was wearing down the board parts. So Piumarta built a lab at NHS that's designed to test every piece of a skateboard. Machines copy the real-world forces that skateboards experience when riders jump, land, and slide along a sidewalk. By smashing and skidding the boards hundreds of times in just a few minutes, he can measure precisely how much each trick breaks them down.

Piumarta tests every part of a skateboard, from the wooden deck to the plastic wheels to the inner metal bearings (rings with rolling balls inside that make it easier for the wheel to spin). These test parts are often destroyed by the time he's done with them—but watching that happen is the whole point.

Once he knows how well a particular part holds up, Piumarta can work with designers and manufacturers to make it stronger, faster, or smoother to ride on. This might mean adjusting the material a part is made of or changing its shape. After more than 40 years, Piumarta still isn't tired of this smashing process: "Every day I walk in and say, 'Oh boy, what are we going to learn today?'"

EARLY SKATEBOARD WHEELS COULD WEAR OUT IN AS LITTLE AS **EIGHT HOURS** OF REAL-WORLD RIDING. THE INVENTION OF **MODERN POLYURETHANE WHEELS** IN THE 1970S HELPED **SAVE THE SPORT.**

Put to the Test

Tim Piumarta uses customized machines that inflict months' worth of wear and tear in just a few minutes. Here are some of the tools he uses to test how skateboards take a beating.

1. Board-breaking machine

An 85-pound (39-kg) anvil slams on the deck of a skateboard in the same place a rider's foot would strike when landing a trick. A good board should withstand at least 100 hits before it cracks.

2. Abrasion machine

A spinning belt of super gritty sandpaper rubs against a skateboard wheel, mimicking months of sliding across pavement. Piumarta weighs the wheel before and after to see how much of it wore away.

3. Wheel dynamometer

A motor revs a wheel up to 300 rotations per minute—about the speed you can reach by pushing off with your feet. Then the wheel "coasts" against a sidewalk-like surface while the machine measures how long it takes to run out of steam.

4. Dust storm in a box

A scratchy powder swirls around the wheel and works its way into the wheel's inner bearings. This simulates months' worth of grime from the ground. Then Piumarta tests the wheel again to learn how much wear was put on the bearings, and how much they slowed down from the test.

SAY "AAAAAH!"

How do TEETH decay?

Chompers. Gnashers. Ivories. Pearly whites. There are lots of funny things to call teeth, but when they fall apart, it's no laughing matter. Tooth decay has harmed humans since prehistoric times, but it's been only relatively recently that we've understood what's happening and how to prevent it. So let's take a closer look at some of the creepier things that can happen inside your mouth—if you're not careful. Open wide!

What are teeth made of **?**

What causes decay **?**

How can you stop it **?**

JUST THE FACTS

Tough Teeth

Teeth aren't bones—they're actually even stronger. And they need to be, considering everything we put them through. Think about it: Every time you crunch a carrot or gnaw on a granola bar, your teeth take on all that smashing and squishing and grinding force without breaking themselves. But as powerful as they are for chomping, teeth can get eaten up by decay if you don't keep them clean.

Rock Hard

Enamel, the shiny white stuff coating the visible part of your teeth, is the hardest substance in your body. It's made mostly of a mineral called apatite, which contains crystals of calcium and other elements. This makes enamel as tough as rocks—literally. But the right combination of factors can wear away the minerals that make up the enamel, the same way wind and water can wear away mountains over time. This gradual process is called decay, and it's how cavities form.

YOU PUT WHAT IN YOUR MOUTH?

These days, dentures to replace missing teeth are typically made of materials like plastic resin. But over the years, people have used some wacky stuff.

Fifteen hundred years ago, the Maya people drilled holes in teeth and filled them with precisely cut precious stones, such as jade. Experts believe this was more for decoration than for dental health.

The Etruscans, who lived in Italy between 800 B.C. and 100 B.C., filled in gaps caused by missing teeth by using gold wire to connect replacement teeth with existing teeth in the mouth.

In the 1850s, denture manufacturers started using vulcanite, an early form of rubber, with teeth made of porcelain. Since these were much more affordable than ivory, false teeth became available to more people who needed them.

By Her Majesty's Royal Letters Patent.
ARTIFICIAL TEETH,
In GOLD, PLATINUM, SILVER, & VULCANITE.

FUN FACT

Prehistoric people GNAWED ON STICKS to keep their teeth clean. An experiment in 2014 showed that chewing sticks from a plant called the NEEM TREE can be just as effective as a MODERN TOOTHBRUSH. But you should still stick to the toothbrush your DENTIST RECOMMENDS.

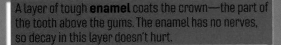

PARTS OF A TOOTH

Decay on the outer layers of a tooth is painless and may go unnoticed.
But once it reaches deep enough, it causes a serious mouth-ache.

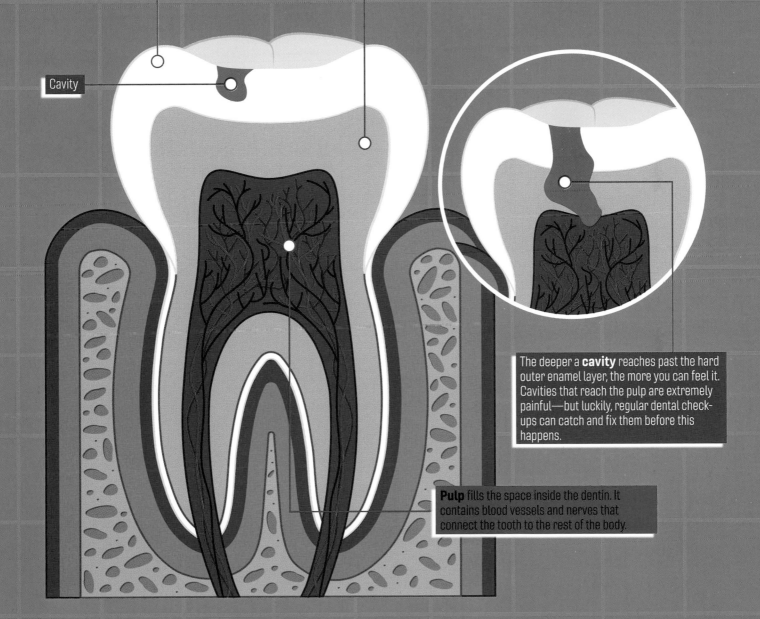

A layer of tough **enamel** coats the crown—the part of the tooth above the gums. The enamel has no nerves, so decay in this layer doesn't hurt.

A layer of bone-like **dentin** makes up most of the tooth. Dentin is strong but slightly squishy to absorb the powerful pressing and grinding forces when we chew food.

Cavity

The deeper a **cavity** reaches past the hard outer enamel layer, the more you can feel it. Cavities that reach the pulp are extremely painful—but luckily, regular dental check-ups can catch and fix them before this happens.

Pulp fills the space inside the dentin. It contains blood vessels and nerves that connect the tooth to the rest of the body.

FUN FACT

>>> When British prime minister WINSTON CHURCHILL started wearing FALSE TEETH at the beginning of WWII, he made sure they were LOOSE FITTING so that he could keep his TRADEMARK LISP.

TELL ME MORE

A HISTORY OF DECAY

Tooth decay has plagued people for millennia. Scientists have found evidence of cavities in the remains of 40,000-year-old Neanderthals! A 5,000-year-old mummy unearthed in Italy also had serious dental problems. Experts think the man's grain-heavy diet was partly to blame. Hard minerals in the grains scratched the surface of his teeth like sandpaper, wearing away the tough enamel—and all the starch (a form of sugar) in the grains didn't help things either. This was a common problem as ancient people started farming grain. Then came refined sugar. In the 1600s, only the wealthy in Europe could afford this imported treat. Kings and queens gorged on sweets at banquets—and their teeth later turned black with cavities. By the mid-1850s, sugar became available to everyone—and unfortunately, so did cavities.

FUN FACTS

>>> As early as about **350 B.C.,** the Greek philosopher **ARISTOTLE** suggested that sweet foods like figs caused **TOOTH DECAY.** But the idea wasn't taken seriously until the 1700s.

>>> If you add up all the time an average person spends **BRUSHING THEIR TEETH,** it would total more than two months throughout their lifetime!

>>> Believe it or not, you're **BORN WITH** the beginnings of all the teeth you'll ever have already nestled **INSIDE YOUR SKULL.**

>>> Most animals **DON'T GET CAVITIES**—they simply don't eat enough **SWEET STUFF.** One exception: **BEARS,** which gorge on **SUGARY BERRIES** before settling in to **HIBERNATE FOR WINTER.**

THE TERROR OF TEETH

Tooth decay is a vicious cycle. Here's how it works.

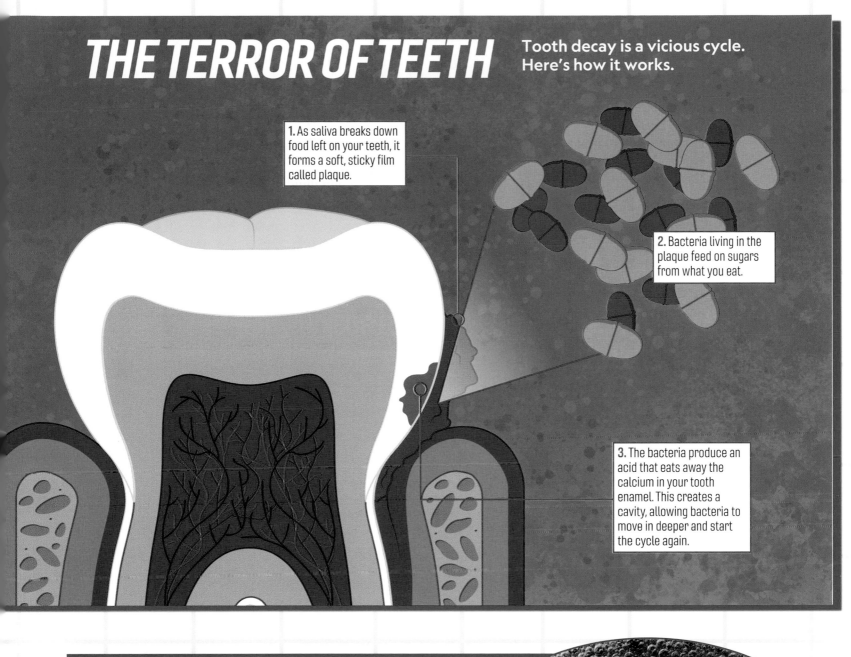

1. As saliva breaks down food left on your teeth, it forms a soft, sticky film called plaque.

2. Bacteria living in the plaque feed on sugars from what you eat.

3. The bacteria produce an acid that eats away the calcium in your tooth enamel. This creates a cavity, allowing bacteria to move in deeper and start the cycle again.

MYTH VERSUS FACT

Will a tooth left in a glass of cola disappear overnight? The concept originated in the 1950s, when a professor testified before the U.S. Congress about the health effects of soft drinks. He said the acid in a cup of cola would dissolve a tooth within two days. The story has stuck around since, but numerous tests have failed to prove it. Sorry, professor, but this one is a myth. Don't get us wrong: Soft drinks still aren't good for your dental health. They contain acids that weaken your tooth enamel and sugars that feed bacteria for a one-two punch of cavity formation. But despite the rumors, a few sips now and then won't melt the teeth out of your mouth, as long as you brush and floss as directed by your dentist.

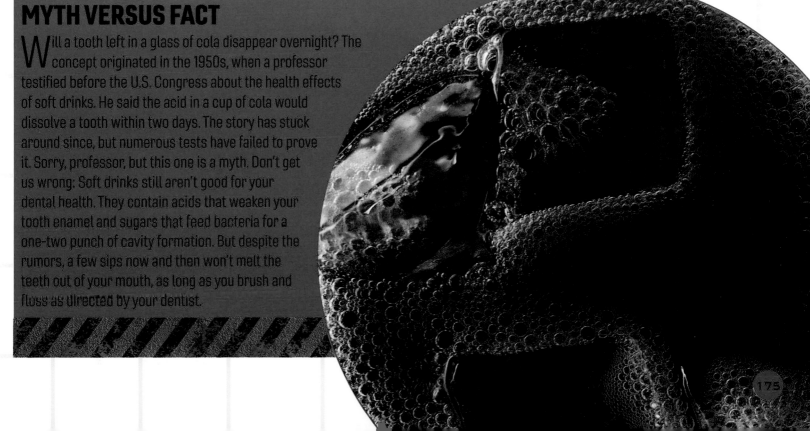

SUPER SKELETON

How do **BONES** break—and help repair themselves?

If you've ever broken a bone, you know it's an awful experience. The pain, the panic—not to mention the boredom of spending weeks or months in a cast while it heals, watching your friends do all the fun things you can't. But what's actually happening when a bone cracks or shatters? Why is that itchy cast even necessary? Strap on your surgical masks, because we're about to peer into your body's deepest depths.

What are bones made of **?**

Why do they break **?**

How do casts help them heal **?**

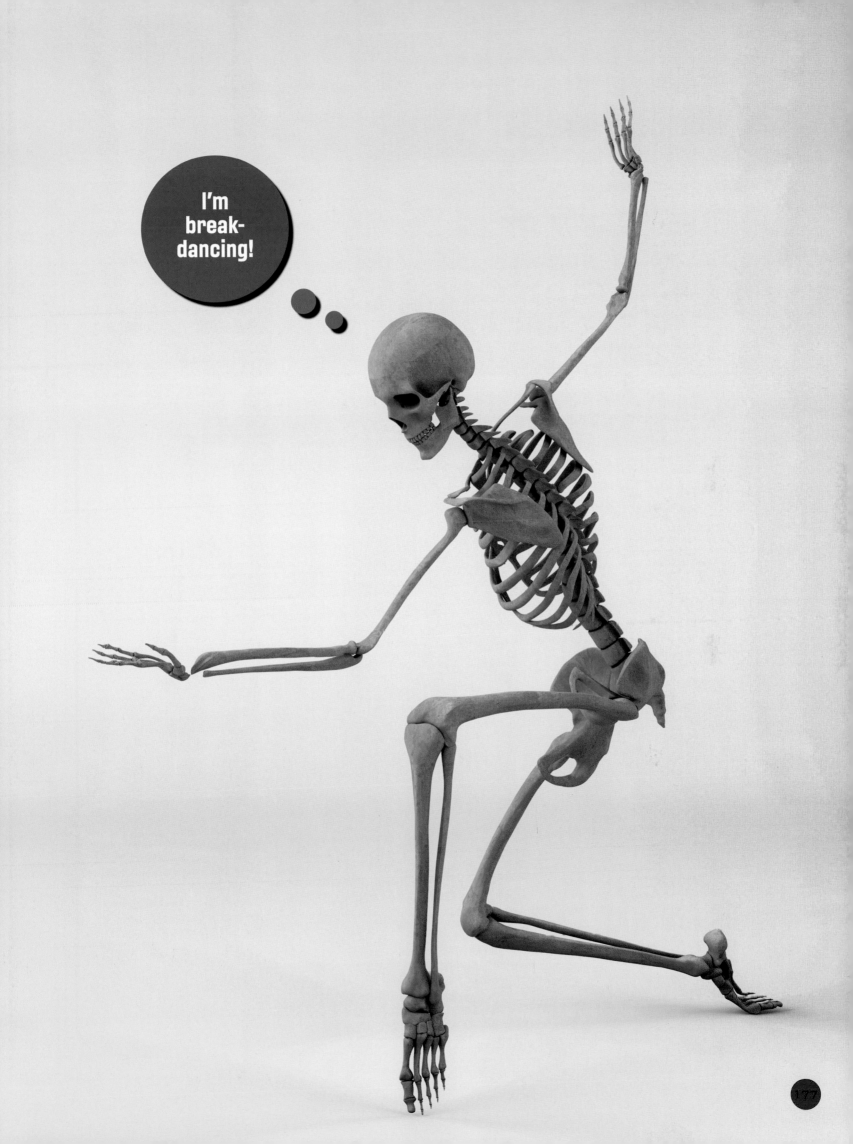

JUST THE FACTS

Bone Breakdown

We humans have more than 200 bones in our bodies. We think of them as hard, but they're mostly made of a spongy material called collagen. Calcium fills in the gaps in the collagen, giving bones their hardness. This mix makes bones strong enough to hold up our bodies, but flexible enough to absorb everyday stresses from all the moving around we do. Every time you take a step, catch a ball, turn a page, or jump for joy, a bone somewhere in your body absorbs some force. But that's exactly the kind of humdrum force your body is built to withstand.

Ouch!

Too much force, though, can overwhelm a bone's tough structure. Bike crashes, bad falls, sports injuries, and other accidents can bend and twist bones more than they can withstand. When this happens, the bone tears apart painfully—often along with the other tissue around it, like muscles and ligaments. This is a break, also called a fracture. The pain is a signal from your body to stop whatever you were doing and get help!

FRACTURE TYPES

The way a bone fractures depends on the strength and direction of the force that's applied to it. Here are some common types.

When something strikes the side of a bone straight on, a **transverse** fracture can result. This type of break cuts directly across a bone the short way.

A strong force from above or below causes an **oblique** fracture that snaps the bone diagonally.

Greenstick fractures happen most often in kids, whose bones are still softer than adults' bones are. The bone bends away from whatever hits it and splinters on the opposite side. But it doesn't break all the way through.

In serious accidents like car crashes, strong forces can come from multiple directions. This can cause **comminuted** fractures, where the bone breaks into three or more pieces.

FUN FACT >>> More than HALF THE BONES in your body are in YOUR HANDS (27 bones each) AND FEET (26).

TELL ME MORE

MENDING THE BREAK

Doctors have many ways of helping broken bones heal, but they all have something in common. Their goal is to get the bones back in the right position so the body's natural healing process can kick in. That's right: As soon as you're injured, your body springs into action to try to fix the damage. The body forms a blood clot called a hematoma to protect the area and starts sending in cells that rebuild the bone bit by bit. It's pretty amazing how much your body can do to repair itself, but don't get the wrong idea: It's still important to get medical treatment for any kind of fracture. If bones aren't set in their proper position, they can heal wrong and get painfully stuck that way.

BACK IN BUSINESS

A broken bone can take anywhere from weeks to months to heal depending on how bad the injury is. Here's how it works.

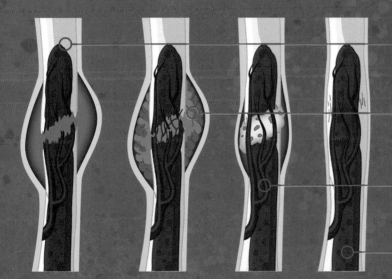

1. Right after the injury, blood rushes into the site of the break. It forms a clot over the fracture and causes swelling that lasts for about a week.

2. Within a few days, the body starts replacing the clot with rubbery cartilage called a callus. Blood vessels grow across the divide as this soft callus holds the bone pieces in place.

3. Over the next few weeks, the soft callus is gradually replaced with a harder callus made of spongy bone tissue.

4. In the final phase, called bone remodeling, hard bone replaces the spongy bone. It can take up to a year for all the swelling to disappear.

PUTTING IT BACK TOGETHER

When you visit the emergency room after a fracture, doctors will likely take an x-ray to see exactly what's going on beneath your skin. The next step is to put the pieces of broken bone back into place. For simple breaks, doctors can often move the bones with their hands from the outside (with plenty of anesthesia to keep you comfortable). For more complicated fractures, they perform surgery to reconnect the bones using metal rods or pins. Once the pieces are aligned correctly, the bone is immobilized, or kept still, with a cast or splint on the outside. This keeps the bone fragments from getting knocked back out of position. Your body is working to stitch them back together, so you want them to stay in the right spot!

METAL DESTROYER

How does RUST eat away iron?

There's something that can silently break apart even the strongest steel and iron. It's ruined bikes, weakened bridges, and brought everything from boats to buildings to their knees. What is this furious force of unbridled chaos? Ready? It's ... rust. No, seriously. Rust might not be the first thing anyone thinks of when it comes to dramatic destruction, but it's a surprisingly pesky problem. To find out how it breaks things down, we're going to get chemical.

How does rust form ?

How does it affect metal ?

How can you prevent it ?

I need to rust for a minute.

JUST THE FACTS

Iron's Enemy

We usually think of iron as one of the toughest things out there. There's even a superhero named after it! But iron has a weakness. Left to its own devices, iron (and steel, which contains iron) will turn reddish-brown, rough, and crumbly with rust. Rust is a type of corrosion, a chemical process that wears away metal. Over time, it can break through boat hulls, destroy the bolts that hold up a building, and even send a steel bridge toppling into the water below.

Rust Recipe

Rust needs three main ingredients to form: iron, water, and oxygen. Other substances (like salt from seawater) can also help things along. As soon as a drop of water hits a piece of iron, it starts a chemical process that forms a small spot of rust on the iron's surface. Then the corrosion starts spreading farther across the object. The thing is, it's not just growing on *top* of the iron—like a tiny chemical zombie, it's actually *changing* the iron into more rust. Eventually, enough rust builds up that it gets flaky and falls off the object. Given enough time, all of the iron can be eaten away.

CORROSIVE COLORS

Rust is just one form of corrosion. Here are a few of its lesser known companions.

Patina turns shiny brown copper a dull green. New York's famous Statue of Liberty started its life the color of a penny, but the salty spray from the water around it turned it the emerald color it is today.

Tarnish turns silver and other metals dingy. Museum workers control heat and humidity to keep precious artifacts from corroding, but they still have to carefully clean off tarnish from time to time.

Combining zinc and copper makes the strong, shiny brass that's used in musical instruments like trumpets. But too much moisture causes dezincification: The zinc wears away, leaving red spots of copper that are easy to break.

FUN FACT >>> The U.S. NAVY spends about THREE BILLION DOLLARS every year fighting RUST and other forms of corrosion.

GETTING RUSTY

As soon as water touches iron, the process of rust formation begins.

1. Water soaks up carbon dioxide from the air. This creates a weak acid, which starts to dissolve the iron.

2. Oxygen from the water combines with the dissolved iron to form iron oxide—otherwise known as rust.

3. The newly formed rust collects into solid particles and deposits itself on the surface of the iron.

4. This process repeats, working its way deeper and deeper into the object as more iron dissolves and more rust forms in its place.

FUN FACT >>> If people didn't keep WORKING to prevent and remove rust on New York City's TRAIN BRIDGES, many of them would CORRODE and fall in only 20 YEARS.

TELL ME MORE

CORROSION CLOSE-UP

Try saying this one out loud: Fe_2O_3. It sounds weird, but it's just the fancy chemist's way of saying "rust." When rust forms, iron (Fe) and oxygen (O) atoms break free from the other atoms they're attached to and combine to form a new compound: iron oxide. One of the reasons rust is so tough to stop is that iron atoms *love* doing this. They're much more comfortable being bound to oxygen than they are hanging around only with other iron atoms. That's why pure iron is extremely rare in nature in the first place: Any bits of it exposed to air and moisture tend to turn rusty the first chance they get.

FUN FACTS

>>> **RUSTY IRON** is responsible for a spooky **RED WATERFALL IN ANTARCTICA,** appropriately named **BLOOD FALLS.** Super-salty water mixes with iron worn away from rocks to give the **SEEPING WATER** its creepy hue.

>>> Steel contains **IRON** and can rust if not treated properly—which is bad news if you're making a building out of it. In the **EARLY 1900s,** before nonrusting stainless steel was invented, people called rust "the great destroyer" or simply **"THE EVIL."**

>>> Iron **RUSTS FASTER** when it's warmer and wetter. A hammer left outside in the **FREEZING-COLD,** dry air of Siberia will take **500 TIMES LONGER** to rust than one in warm, rainy Panama.

>>> Rust takes up **MORE SPACE** than the iron it replaces. This means that **WHEN MACHINES GET RUSTY,** the corrosion can **CLOG THEIR PARTS** and make them more difficult to move.

Rusty, reddish-brown water pours out of Taylor Glacier.

BUSTING RUST

One way workers can remove rust is through electrolysis, which uses electric current. Here's how it breaks down.

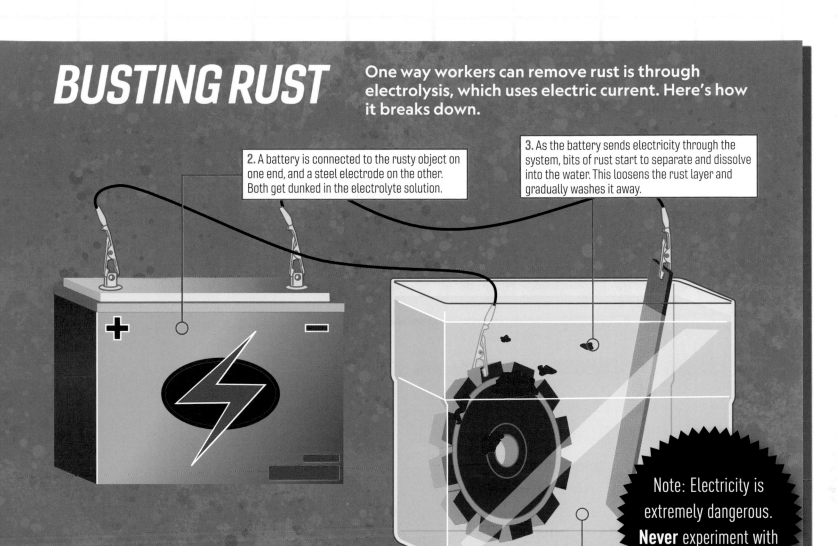

2. A battery is connected to the rusty object on one end, and a steel electrode on the other. Both get dunked in the electrolyte solution.

3. As the battery sends electricity through the system, bits of rust start to separate and dissolve into the water. This loosens the rust layer and gradually washes it away.

Note: Electricity is extremely dangerous. **Never** experiment with electricity.

1. A bucket filled with water and a soapy compound called sodium carbonate, or washing soda, creates an electrolyte—a solution that an electric charge can move through.

PUTTING IT BACK TOGETHER

Can you unrust a rusty metal part—or keep it from rusting in the first place? We'll start with the bad news: Unless you have some serious mad-scientist equipment, it's almost impossible to turn rust back into pure iron. (It really wants to be rust, remember?) But if the rusting process is caught soon enough, it can still be stopped for a while. A good scraping will remove the layer of rusty buildup , and so will a process known as electrolysis. Then a fresh coat of paint, or another material that seals out moisture and oxygen, can keep the corrosion from starting again immediately. Eventually, though, paint flakes off or wears down. Sooner or later, rust finds a way.

ALL BACKED UP

Why do TOILETS clog?

What's something you use every day and can find at home, at school, or on vacation? Something you probably don't think about much when it's working, but that your life would get pretty nasty without? We're talking, of course, about the toilet! These everyday wonders of sanitation allow us to do our business and then go about our day—well, usually. What happens when this system breaks down? Hold your nose, because we're about to go there.

How do toilets clog **?**

What can clog them **?**

How do you fix the problem **?**

JUST THE FACTS

Toilet Talk

Have you thanked a toilet today? Seriously. We take them for granted, but they're often considered one of the most important inventions of all time. By carrying our waste away through a sewer to somewhere it can be safely treated, flushing toilets help keep our homes clean and prevent the spread of diseases. Without these shiny marvels of engineering, modern cities couldn't be built.

Feeling Flushed

One of many brilliant things about toilets: They operate entirely without electricity. Instead, they use water pressure and gravity to get the job done. The trick is a specially shaped tube called a P trap (no giggling—it's named for its shape). When you flush, water plunges into the bowl from the tank above, forcing what's already in the bowl over a curved section of pipe. On the other side of the curve, gravity pulls it back down, creating a siphon that sucks down the rest of the bowl contents. But if something clogs the P trap (hey, we said no giggling!), it's harder for this siphon to form. The once mighty toilet is temporarily reduced to a useless hunk of porcelain—one that comes with a disgusting risk of overflow.

TOILET TIMELINE

The toilet has a long—and sometimes smelly—history.

CIRCA 3100 B.C.: Ancient Egyptians fill clay pots with sand and use them as indoor toilets. (It's basically a litter box for humans!)

CIRCA A.D. 500: Chinese people start producing soft paper that people use for post-toilet wiping—the world's first TP.

500–1500: Medieval Europeans dispose of waste in shared open pits called cesspools. Not only do these breed disease, but they also get very stinky.

1596: The first flushing toilet is invented for England's Queen Elizabeth I by her godson, Sir John Harington. He publishes instructions for how to build more, but almost nobody does.

1775: British inventor Alexander Cumming patents a flush toilet with a curved pipe to keep sewer smells from wafting back into the bathroom. After other inventors improve the design, it begins to catch on.

1834: The first public toilets are built in France for men who need to go on the go. The facilities are installed on city streets, in railroad stations, and in stores.

1880s: Factories in Europe and the U.S. start mass-producing flush toilets, making them more affordable to everyone.

BIG BLOCKAGE

The P trap (OK, fine, go ahead and giggle) is the most common place in a toilet for clogs to form. Here's what happens.

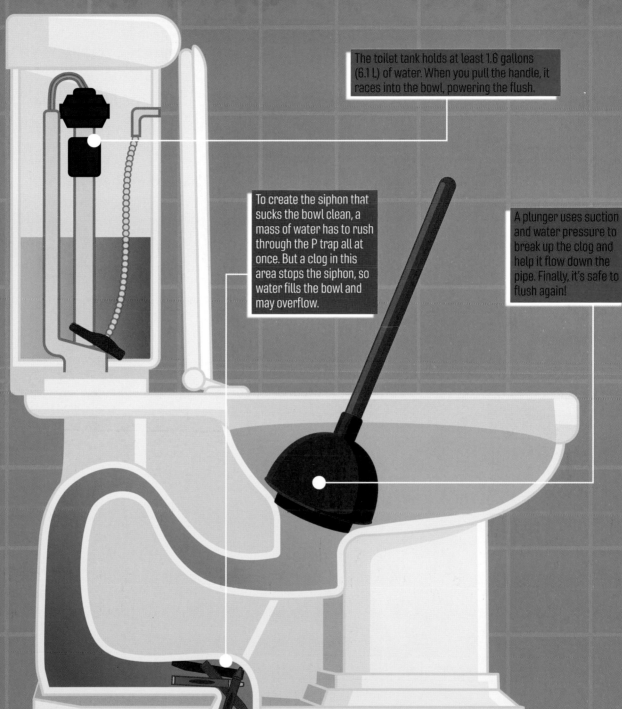

The toilet tank holds at least 1.6 gallons (6.1 L) of water. When you pull the handle, it races into the bowl, powering the flush.

To create the siphon that sucks the bowl clean, a mass of water has to rush through the P trap all at once. But a clog in this area stops the siphon, so water fills the bowl and may overflow.

A plunger uses suction and water pressure to break up the clog and help it flow down the pipe. Finally, it's safe to flush again!

FUN FACT >>> In 2018, a TOILET COMPANY was forced to recall more than 1.4 MILLION flushing devices. The problem? A valve in the system sometimes built up TOO MUCH PRESSURE, causing the whole toilet tank to EXPLODE.

TELL ME MORE

What makes toilets clog? We know what you might be thinking: too much poo. But natural waste usually isn't the problem. Instead, the problem involves stuff like napkins, cotton swabs, diapers, and wet wipes. These products are made of tough fibers that don't break down easily in water. This makes it more likely for them to stick in the trap and block the flow for everything else. Too much toilet paper can also be a problem. It's thin enough to fall apart in water, but balling up a whole fistful can still overpower a flush. Toys and crayons thrown in by pesky younger siblings are also common clog causes. Basically, anything except your bodily products and a little bit of TP shouldn't go down the bowl!

FUN FACTS

>>> The average adult puts out **1,110 POUNDS** (503 kg) of urine and **353 POUNDS** (160 kg) of solid waste every year. No wonder we need **SEWERS** to take it all away.

>>> Contrary to popular myth, the English plumber **THOMAS CRAPPER** did not invent **THE TOILET.** The name is just a **COINCIDENCE**—we swear.

>>> In 2012, the city of **SUWON,** South Korea, opened the world's first **TOILET THEME PARK.** The Restroom Cultural Park features an array of **TOILET STYLES** for visitors to admire, along with a giant toilet-shaped building.

TRY THIS!

To flush or not to flush? Grab a few squares of toilet paper and a paper towel. Place each in a separate bowl and then pour in water to fill the bowls about halfway. Stir the water and paper gently with a spoon, let sit for two minutes, then stir again. Did any of the paper break down? What happened to the paper towel? You can probably guess which one is more likely to clog a P trap (or any drain).

TAKING THE PLUNGE

A plunger forces water back and forth through the toilet trap to blast a clog apart.

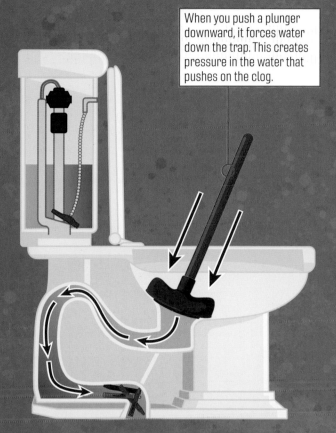

When you push a plunger downward, it forces water down the trap. This creates pressure in the water that pushes on the clog.

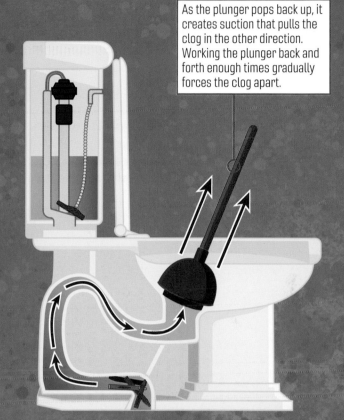

As the plunger pops back up, it creates suction that pulls the clog in the other direction. Working the plunger back and forth enough times gradually forces the clog apart.

IT'S KIND OF A FUNNY STORY ...

Next time your toilet backs up, remember that it could be worse—WAY worse. In 2017, sanitation workers in London dealt with a monster clog that blocked an entire underground sewer pipe. The culprit: a 143-ton (130-t) glob of diapers, bandages, food waste, and cooking fat that thousands of people had flushed down their toilets and kitchen sinks. The crud congealed into a rock-solid mass called a "fatberg" that weighed almost as much as a blue whale. It stretched 820 feet (250 m) through the pipe, making it longer than London's famous Tower Bridge. To clear the clog, workers used high-pressure hoses to blast the stinking mass apart. They could only get through about 22 to 33 tons (20 to 30 t) of the material a day.

Workers in London are constantly battling massive fatbergs.

>>>LESSON LEARNED!
THE GREAT STINK
SUMMER 1858

The Incident

It was a particularly sweltering summer in London. A heat wave raised temperatures in the city above 90 degrees Fahrenheit (32°C). The heat itself was unpleasant enough, especially as thousands of newcomers looking for jobs made London more crowded. But soon an even greater annoyance spread through the city: the sickening odor of hot, steaming human waste.

The stench lasted for months, making people all over London feel ill. It wafted over city streets and followed people into their homes and places of work. It got so bad that Parliament had to cancel sessions after lawmakers fled the building, desperately covering their noses with handkerchiefs. One city leader called the smelly summer an "unbearable horror." An editorial in a London newspaper was more to the point: "It stinks!"

What Went Wrong

A heat wave set off this stinky situation, but it was decades in the making. Between 1800 and 1850, London's population more than doubled as people moved there from the countryside to find work. The city's sewage system wasn't equipped to handle the growing population and all their bodily waste.

Most of the city didn't have indoor plumbing. Instead, people collected their waste and poured it into outdoor cesspools, which workers had to empty with shovels and buckets every night. Then they carted it to the countryside to sell to farmers as fertilizer. But as the city grew, the shovelers couldn't keep up, and cesspools started overflowing into the Thames River. Wealthier households had flush toilets, but with no real sewer system, these ultimately washed waste into the river as well.

The result was a river full of terrible sludge that it carried through the city. And as soon as the heat wave hit, it turned into a simmering brew of number two, sending its nasty vapors far and wide.

Cartoons from 1858 show London's River Thames as a dirty old man (with politicians trying to make him look cleaner) and the River Styx (a river in the underworld from Greek mythology).

THE BIG TAKEAWAY

THE GREAT STINK WAS UNDENIABLY MISERABLE. But thanks to Londoners' disgusting experience that summer, a better system is available to us today. Fed up with the smell—and the complaints of constituents—Britain's Parliament fast-tracked a bill to fund the construction of a massive new sewer system. Engineers spent the next several years building 82 miles (132 km) of underground pipes that carried waste safely out of the city and kept it out of the water supply. The lesson? Sometimes, if you want things to change, you really have to make a stink.

TOILETS FOR ALL

DESPITE **TECHNOLOGICAL ADVANCES** IN **TOILETRY,** NOT EVERYBODY HAS ONE. **UP TO 4.5 BILLION PEOPLE—** MORE THAN HALF THE WORLD'S POPULATION— STILL DON'T HAVE **SAFE PLACES TO GO.**

THE PROBLEM:

Sewer systems like this one, built in London after the Great Stink, aren't possible everywhere. In many poor or war-torn areas, there are no clean water or sewage systems. Waste ends up in drinking water and makes millions of people sick.

THE SOLUTION:

To help, many engineers are working on new types of toilets that compost waste or otherwise safely dispose of it—all without being connected to running water. Toilets like this one use chemicals in the space beneath the toilet seat to help partially disinfect waste and reduce odors. With hundreds of years of failures to learn from, there's hope that things will improve.

TRY THIS!

A BIT RUSTY

DISCOVER HOW TO MAKE RUST—AND STOP IT FROM FORMING IN THE FIRST PLACE

Steel yourself—this is going to get a little gritty. Most engineers will tell you that making rust is not at the top of their list of things to do. *Preventing* it is. But since rust has been a problem for people since, well, the Iron Age, it's important to get up close and personal with the brownish-orange stuff to watch it form and learn how to stop it. Where does it come from? What makes a good environment for it, and what stops it in its tracks?

WHAT YOU NEED

TIME: About 15 minutes to set up, then two to three days to observe

1. 3 small jars

2. Masking tape

3. Permanent marker

4. Salt (1 teaspoon/5 mL)

5. 3 pieces of steel wool

6. Rubber gloves

7. Vegetable oil (about ¼ cup/59 mL)

WHAT TO DO

1. Using a permanent marker and masking tape, create labels for your jars so that you have jar 1, jar 2, and jar 3.

2. Fill each jar about a third full with water. To jar 2, add the salt, then stir to dissolve.

3. Using rubber gloves, place a piece of steel wool in each jar.

4. In jar 3, top with the vegetable oil (add enough to make sure any steel wool sticking out of the water is completely covered).

5. Leave the jars out on the counter for two to three days, then record your observations.

You don't want to get rust in your body, so don't touch the rusty steel wool with your bare hands. Use rubber gloves, and ask an adult for help with cleanup.

WHAT TO EXPECT

JAR 2 SHOULD HAVE THE MOST RUST DEVELOPING ON IT, WHILE JAR 3 SHOULD HAVE THE LEAST. JAR 1 SHOULD ALSO HAVE BEGUN TO RUST.

WHAT'S GOING ON?

THE CHEMICAL REACTION THAT MAKES RUST NEEDS A FEW INGREDIENTS: IRON, WATER, AND OXYGEN. STEEL—AND STEEL WOOL—IS MADE MOSTLY OF IRON, SO IT TENDS TO RUST. IN JAR 1, THE CONDITIONS WERE RIGHT FOR THE IRON IN THE STEEL WOOL TO BEGIN TRADING ATOMS WITH THE OXYGEN AROUND IT, LEADING TO IRON OXIDE, OR RUST. WHEN THERE'S SALT IN WATER, THE WATER BECOMES MORE CONDUCTIVE, MEANING IT'S EASIER FOR IRON AND OXYGEN ATOMS TO MOVE AROUND AND TRADE PLACES—THAT'S WHY THERE'S MORE RUST IN JAR 2. THE OIL IN JAR 3, ON THE OTHER HAND, PREVENTS OXYGEN FROM REACHING THE STEEL WOOL, MAKING IT HARDER FOR RUST TO FORM.

GLOSSARY

ablative—evaporates or melts when exposed to extreme heat

aerial—done in the air

anesthesia—medically induced loss of feeling in a person's body

atom—the smallest bit of something; the basic building block of matter

ballast—heavy material used to make something stable

buoyancy—an object's ability to float in a fluid

cantilever—a structure that sticks out from another structure to support something above it

circuit—a path along which an electric current travels

compress—to press or squeeze something to make it smaller

conduct—to allow something, like heat or electricity, to move from one place to another

contracting—becoming or being made into something smaller

debris—the scattered pieces left after something has been destroyed

density—the amount of mass in a certain amount of an object or area

dissolve—to mix into and become part of the liquid

electron—a very small *particle* of matter that has a negative charge and travels around the nucleus (center part) of an *atom*

erode—to wear away or slowly be destroyed, often by natural forces

fault—a break between rock formations in Earth's crust where *tectonic plates* move

footprint—the area covered by something, such as a building's base

fracture—a crack or break

friction—a force that slows a moving object when it touches another object

glacier—a huge mass of ice that moves slowly over land

helium—the second-lightest gas and element after *hydrogen*

hydraulic—moved by or using the pressure of liquid

hydrogen—a gas that has no color or smell; the simplest, lightest, and most common element

ignited—set on fire

inert—does not react chemically

inertia—a measure of how difficult it is to change an object's state of motion—that is, to move if it's still or change the way it's moving if it's in motion

karst—landscape made up of soft rock (like

limestone) that can *erode* away, allowing sinkholes, underground streams, and caverns to form

kinetic energy—the energy of motion

liquefaction—the changing of solid soil into a liquid mass during an earthquake

lithosphere—the outer part of Earth's surface, about 60 miles (100 km) deep

mantle—Earth's middle layer, between the crust and the core

microorganism—an extremely small living thing, visible only with a microscope

migrate—to move from one area to another on a regular basis

particles—the very small parts that make up matter, such as an *atom*

piston—a part of an engine that moves up and down inside a hollow tube, putting pressure on other parts of the engine and causing them to move

pixels—small dots that form the picture on a television screen, computer monitor, etc.

plague—a large number of harmful or annoy-ing things

plate boundary—the spot where two or more *tectonic plates* meet

potential energy—stored-up energy

pressurized—when more pressure is put on something inside a container than there is outside of it, or in spaceflight, when the pressure inside a container is the same as the air pressure on Earth

resistance—a stopping or slowing force in movement, or how much something can push back on an electric current passing through it

rigid—not easy to bend

rivets—metal bolts or pins used to hold pieces of metal together

secrete—to produce and give off a substance

siphon—a tube that liquid moves up and down through, often using air pressure

snowpack—a dense pile of slow-melting snow

swarm—a large group of something, such as insects, moving together

trusses—sturdy frames made of beams, bars, or rods that support a roof or bridge

tectonic plates—enormous moving slabs of the Earth's crust

tension—a stretching force

tremor—the shaking of the ground before or after an earthquake

SELECT BIBLIOGRAPHY

BOOKS FOR KIDS

Callery, Sean. *50 Things You Should Know About Titanic.* QEB Publishing, 2016.

Carson, Mary Kay. *The Tornado Scientist: Seeing Inside Severe Storms.* Houghton Mifflin Harcourt, 2019.

Cobb, Vicki. *Fireworks: Where's the Science Here?* Millbrook Press, 2006.

Connolly, Sean. *Massively Epic Engineering Disasters: 33 Thrilling Experiments Based on History's Greatest Blunders.* Workman Publishing, 2017.

DK. *Human Body!* DK Publishing, 2017.

Drimmer, Stephanie Warren. *Ultimate Weatherpedia.* National Geographic, 2019.

Graham, Ian. *You Wouldn't Want to Be on the Hindenburg!* Franklin Watts, 2008.

Macdonald, Fiona. *You Wouldn't Want to Live Without Toilets!* Franklin Watts, 2015.

Mattern, Joann. *Bridges (Engineering Wonders).* Rourke Educational Media, 2016.

Otfinoski, Steven. *Avalanches.* Children's Press, 2016.

Reeder, Eric. *Natural Phenomena: Sinkholes.* Focus Readers, 2019.

Squire, Ann O. *Sinkholes.* Children's Press, 2016.

BOOKS FOR ADULTS

Ashton, Rosemary. *One Hot Summer: Dickens, Darwin, Disraeli, and the Great Stink of 1858.* Yale University Press, 2017.

Black + Decker. *The Complete Guide to Plumbing,* updated 7th ed. Quarto Publishing, 2019.

Blockley, David. *Bridges: The Science and Art of the World's Most Inspiring Structures.* Oxford University Press, 2010.

Byles, Jeff. *Rubble: Unearthing the History of Demolition.* Harmony Books, 2005.

DeVries, Kelly, and Robert D. Smith. *Medieval Weapons: An Illustrated History of Their Impact.* ABC-CLIO, 2007.

Diven, Richard J., and Mark Shaurette. *Demolition: Practices, Technology, and Management.* Purdue University Press, 2010.

Eng, Ronald C., ed. *Mountaineering: The Freedom of the Hills,* 8th ed. Mountaineers Books, 2010.

Fountain, Henry. *The Great Quake: How the Biggest Earthquake in North America Changed Our Understanding of the Planet.* Crown, 2017.

Lehner, Mark. *The Complete Pyramids: Solving the Ancient Mysteries.* Thames and Hudson, 2008.

Levy, Matthys, and Mario Salvadori. *Why Buildings Fall Down.* W. W. Norton and Company, 1992.

Liss, Helene. *Demolition: The Art of Demolishing, Dismantling, Imploding, Toppling & Razing.* Black Dog and Leventhal, 2000.

Lockwood, Jeffrey A. *Locust: The Devastating Rise and Mysterious Disappearance of the Insect That Shaped the American Frontier.* Basic Books, 2004.

Lucsko, David N. *Junkyards, Gearheads, and Rust: Salvaging the Automotive Past.* Johns Hopkins University Press, 2016.

Molnar, Peter. *Plate Tectonics: A Very Short Introduction.* Oxford University Press, 2015.

Newman, James A. *Modern Sports Helmets: Their History, Science, and Art.* Schiffer Publishing, 2007.

Petroski, Henry. *To Engineer Is Human: The Role of Failure in Successful Design.* Vintage Books, 1992.

Puleo, Stephen. *Dark Tide: The Great Boston Molasses Flood of 1919.* Beacon Press, 2003.

Ratay, Robert T. *Forensic Structural Engineering Handbook.* McGraw Hill, 2000.

Rubin, Susan Goldman. *Toilets, Toasters, and Telephones: The How and Why of Everyday Objects.* Browndeer Press, 1998.

Ruth, Brian J. *Chainsaw Manual for Homeowners: Learn to Safely Use Your Saw to Trim Trees, Cut Firewood, and Fell Trees.* Fox Chapel Publishing, 2018.

Shlager, Neil, ed. *When Technology Fails: Significant Technological Disasters, Accidents, and Failures of the Twentieth Century.* Gale Research, 1994.

Ungar, Peter S. *Teeth: A Very Short Introduction.* Oxford University Press, 2014.

Waldman, Jonathan. *Rust: The Longest War.* Simon and Schuster, 2015.

Wright, A., and P. G. Newbery. *Electric Fuses,* 3rd ed. Institution of Engineering and Technology, 2004.

WEBSITES

Grown-ups: Kids can learn more about how things work at these sites:

Adventures in Chemistry

Britannica Online

Controlled Demolition Inc.

Guinness World Records

How Stuff Works

NASA

National Geographic Kids

Smithsonian Magazine

FIND OUT MORE!

BOOKS

Demolition: The Art of Demolishing, Dismantling, Imploding, Toppling & Razing
By Helene Liss
(Black Dog and Leventhal, 2000)
Go behind the scenes to discover incredible implosions and destructive demolitions.

Massively Epic Engineering Disasters: 33 Thrilling Experiments Based on History's Greatest Blunders
By Sean Connolly
(Workman, 2017)
Use cool experiments to learn about amazing engineering failures.

Science: A Visual Encyclopedia
By the Smithsonian Institution
(DK Publishers, 2014)
A wide-ranging look at many areas of science, great discoveries, and scientists.

Try This! 50 Fun Experiments for the Mad Scientist in You
By Karen Romano Young
(National Geographic Kids, 2014)
Fun hands-on science for young explorers.

Ultimate Weatherpedia
By Stephanie Warren Drimmer
(National Geographic Kids, 2019)
Learn how weather happens and experience the world's most extreme weather.

VIDEOS

Adults, you can learn more about these topics from the book with online videos.

Britannica Kids

Controlled Demolition Inc.

The Great Stink

Guinness World Records

Loma Prieta Earthquake

Ohio Demolition Disaster

San Diego Fireworks Fail

Tacoma Narrows Bridge Collapse

Check out the How Things Work series on the National Geographic Kids YouTube channel.

INDEX

Boldface indicates illustrations.

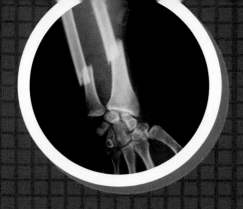

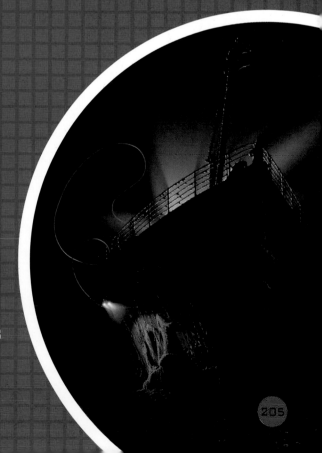

CREDITS

All artwork and diagrams by Lachina, unless otherwise noted below.

AD: Adobe Stock; ASP: Alamy Stock Photo; GI: Getty Images; SCI: Science Source; SS: Shutterstock

4, Supachai/AD; 5 (UP), Sollina Images/GI; 5 (LO), FotoYakov/SS; 6 (LE), sabelskaya/AD; 6 (CTR), Andrew Paterson/ASP; 6 (RT), Adrienne Loizeaux Grant/Controlled Demolition, Inc.; 7 (UP LE), tapong117/AD; 7 (UP RT), Adrienne Loizeaux Grant/Controlled Demolition, Inc.; 7 (RT), mihail/AD; 7 (LO LE); guy harrop/ASP; 7 (LO RT), IIHS; **CHAPTER 1:** 11, Casarsa/GI; 12, Luke Schmidt/SS; 14 (LE), Ozimages/ASP; 14 (RT), sabelskaya/AD; 14 (LO RT), Micah Schmidt; 15 (LO), AfriPics.com/ASP; 16, Adrienne Loizeaux Grant/Controlled Demolition, Inc.; 17 (UP LE), Charles D. Winters/SCI; 17 (remaining), Adrienne Loizeaux Grant/Controlled Demolition, Inc.; 19, sonsedskaya/AD; 20 (UP), Michael Marfell/GI; 20 (L), George Doyle/GI; 20 (RT), AyhanTuran Menekay/ SS; 22 (LE) Tina/AD; 22 (RT), Andrew Paterson/ASP; 23 (LO), Monty Rakusen/GI; 25, simonkr/GI; 27 (RT), jobi_pro/AD; 27 (LO), Кирилл Рыжов/AD; 29, Elizabeth W. Kearley/GI; 30 (UP), Scrudje/AD; 30 (LE), Danita Delimont/ASP; 30 (LO LE), Hemis/ASP; 30 (LO RT), ferkhova/AD; 30 (RT),

PRISMA ARCHIVO/ASP; 32 (UP), Wolfgang/AD; 32 (LO), Micah Schmidt; 33, GL Archive/ASP; 34, Bill Lackey; 35 (UP), bob the builder/ASP; 35 (LO), David Guralnick/Detroit News via AP; 37, lloyd/SS; 38 (UP), Vince Padilla/SS; 38 (LO), Thomas Winz/GI; 40 (UP), Sheila Fitzgerald/SS; 40 (CTR), Kevin P. Coughlin/Office of Governor Andrew M. Cuomo; 40 (LO), ketkata leejungphemphoon/SS; 41, JackF/ADs; 42, Micah Schmidt; 43, Micah Schmidt; **CHAPTER 2:** 47, Caspar Benson/GI; 48, IIHS; 49, Vintage Archives/ASP; 50 (LE), Volvo Car Corporation; 50 (UP RT), Adhitama/SS; 50 (RT), Patti McConville/ASP; 50 (LO RT), Micah Schmidt; 51, Bhakpong/ADs; 52-53, IIHS; 55, praphab144/AD; 57 (UP), Piotr/AD; 57 (CTR), Richard /SS; 57 (LO), jdwfoto/AD; 59, Maui01 /GI; 60 (LE), Jasmin Pawlowicz/SS; 60 (RT), PaoloBruschi/SS; 60 (LO LE), Epic Fireworks; 60 (LO RT), EyeEm/ASP; 62 (UP), South China Morning Post/GI; 62 (LO LE), ldambies/SS; 62 (LO RT), Steve Caulk; 63, watchara/AD; 64, ZUMA Press Inc/ASP; 65 (UP), Ian Georgeson/ASP; 65 (LO), benjaminjk/AD; 67, smrm1977/SS; 69, Nor Gal/SS; 71, Sonsedska/GI; 72 (LE), Haitong Yu/GI; 72 (RT), Darryl Pitt/Macovich Collection of Meteorites; 72 (LO), Ria Novosti/SCI; 74 (LE), REUTERS/ASP; 74 (RT), NASA/Johns Hopkins APL/Ed

Whitman; 76 (LE), Micah Schmidt; 76 (RT), Stuart Fuidge/SS; 76 (LO RT), Coprid/ AD; 77, Micah Schmidt; **CHAPTER 3:** 81, the_lightwriter/AD; 82 (LE), Popperfoto/GI; 82 (LO LE), Pictorial Press Ltd/ASP; 82 (RT), Science History Images/ASP; 72 (LO RT), SSPL/GI; 84 (UP), Drozhzhina Elena/SS; 84 (LE), UtCon Collection/ASP; 84 (LO), Coprid/AD; 85, Ken Marschall; 87, Lukas/AD; 88, the_lightwriter/AD; 90-91, Jahan Rasty; 93, peepo/GI; 95 (UP), NBCUniversal/GI; 95 (CTR), Lockheed Martin; 95 (LO), joebelanger/GI; 96 (UP), Tacoma Public Library; 96 (LO LE), Library of Congress; 96 (LO RT), Library of Congress; 97, Tacoma Public Library; 99, qoppi/SS; 100 (CTR), Florilegius/ASP; 100 (LO), guy harrop/ASP; 103 (UP RT), Sarah2/SS; 103 (LE), David Nunuk/SCI; 103 (RT), Lifestyle Travel Photo/SS; 103 (LO RT), Hulton Archive/GI; 105, Volodymyr Tverdokhlibt/SS; 106 (LO), ZUMA Press Inc/ASP; 106 (RT), Star Tribune/GI; 108 (UP RT), Matyas Rehak/SS; 108 (RT), Ratthaphong Ekariyasap/SS; 108 (LO LE), Micah Schmidt; 109, Inti St Clair/GI; 111, Givaga/ADs; 112 (LE), AlexAnton/SS; 112 (LO LE), Martchan/SS; 112 (UP RT), Punnawit Suwattananun/ SS; 112 (RT), Barna Tanko/SS; 112 (LO RT), WitR/SS; 114-115 (LO), Vitaly Korovin/SS; 115 (UP), Sergey-73/SS; 115

For David, who can fix anything. —MG

Since 1888, the National Geographic Society has funded more than 14,000 research, conservation, education, and storytelling projects around the world. National Geographic Partners distributes a portion of the funds it receives from your purchase to National Geographic Society to support programs including the conservation of animals and their habitats. To learn more, visit natgeo.com/info.

For more information, visit nationalgeographic.com, call 1-877-873-6846, or write to the following address:

National Geographic Partners, LLC
1145 17th Street NW
Washington, DC 20036-4688 U.S.A.

For librarians and teachers: nationalgeographic.com/books/librarians-and-educators

More for kids from National Geographic: natgeokids.com

National Geographic Kids magazine inspires children to explore their world with fun yet educational articles on animals, science, nature, and more. Using fresh storytelling and amazing photography, Nat Geo Kids shows kids ages 6 to 14 the fascinating truth about the world—and why they should care. **natgeo.com/subscribe**

For rights or permissions inquiries, please contact National Geographic Books Subsidiary Rights:
bookrights@natgeo.com

Library of Congress Cataloging-in-Publication Data

Names: Grunbaum, Mara, author.
Title: Break down : a how things work look at how they don't / by Mara Grunbaum.
Description: Washington D.C. : National Geographic, 2022. | Includes bibliographical references and index. | Audience: Ages 8-12 | Audience: Grades 4-6
Identifiers: LCCN 2021019635 | ISBN 9781426373053 (hardcover) | ISBN 9781426373060 (library binding)
Subjects: LCSH: Structural failures--Juvenile literature. | Failure analysis (Engineering)--Juvenile literature. | Wrecking--Juvenile literature.
Classification: LCC TA656 .G78 2022 | DDC 620.1--dc23
LC record available at https://lccn.loc.gov/2021019635

Acknowledgments

The publisher wishes to thank the Girl Friday Productions team for their hard work on this book: Leah Jenness and Emilie Sandoz-Voyer, Paul Barrett, Micah Schmidt, and Dave Valencia; and the National Geographic Kids team: Shelby Lees, senior editor; Julide Dengel, senior designer; Sarah J. Mock, senior photo editor; Joan Gossett, senior manager, managing editorial; and Anne LeongSon and Gus Tello, associate designers.

Printed in China
22/PPS/1

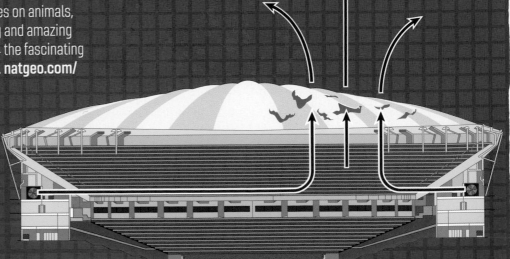